# RESEARCH
# STRATEGIES
# FOR
# SECONDARY
# DATA

*This book is dedicated to my wife*
*Beverly M. Brown*
*and*
*my two sons and their wonderful wives*
*Brian Riedel and Lynne McBride*
*Eric and Aylin Riedel*

# RESEARCH STRATEGIES FOR SECONDARY DATA

A Perspective
for Criminology and
Criminal Justice

## MARC RIEDEL

Sage Publications, Inc.
*International Educational and Professional Publisher*
Thousand Oaks ■ London ■ New Delhi

*For information:*

Sage Publications, Inc.
2455 Teller Road
Thousand Oaks, California 91320
E-mail: order@sagepub.com

Sage Publications Ltd.
6 Bonhill Street
London EC2A 4PU
United Kingdom

Sage Publications India Pvt. Ltd.
M-32 Market
Greater Kailash I
New Delhi 110 048 India

Printed in the United States of America

*Library of Congress Cataloging-in-Publication Data*

Riedel, Marc.
  Research strategies for secondary data : A perspective for criminology and criminal justice / by Marc Riedel.
      p.   cm.
Includes bibliographical references and index.
  ISBN 0-8039-5837-4 — ISBN 0-8039-5838-2
  I. Title.  1.  Criminology—United States. 2.  Criminal justice, Administration of—United States.
  HV6025 .R585 1999
  364.973—dc21                                           99-006836

This book is printed on acid-free paper.


00   01   02   03   04   05   06   7   6   5   4   3   2   1


*Acquisition Editor:*     Kassie Gavrilis
*Editorial Assistant:*    Anna Howland
*Production Editor:*      Astrid Virding
*Editorial Assistant:*    Cindy Bear
*Typesetter:*             Christina M. Hill
*Cover Designer:*         Ravi Balasuriya

# CONTENTS

# FOREWORD

Researchers use data originally collected for other purposes all the time. For example, the U.S. Census of Population is mandated by the Constitution as a count of people in the nation, but the Census is used by researchers for far more than merely counting people. The Uniform Crime Reporting program provides measures of serious crimes reported to police across all 50 states and the District of Columbia, but researchers do much more with the crime rates than list them for each jurisdiction. They examine patterns of crime rates across places in relation to trends in other characteristics.

Generally speaking, when data originally collected for one purpose are used for other research, the data are often referred to as secondary data. But there is nothing "secondary" about the research undertaken with such data or about the analytical techniques applied to such data. In this book, Marc Riedel describes the research processes and activities that are involved in research that relies upon secondary data. He shows that the research accomplished with secondary data can be groundbreaking research or extremely important policy research. He also shows that secondary analysis of previously collected data often involves the use of newly applied statistical analysis techniques that reveal new findings. In short, there is nothing "secondary" about pursuing research with secondary data.

In this book, Riedel reveals that conducting research with secondary data has its own set of research activities, techniques, and arts. It requires detailed knowledge about sources of secondary data. It requires creative vision to see how the data can address theoretically or policy-driven research issues and questions. It requires the ability to negotiate with and persuade agency executives to release data for further analysis. It requires all the skill and knowledge involved in developing and executing a research design and data analysis plan. It often requires the design of a data collection plan and data coding forms, because secondary data may have to be extracted from agency files. Sometimes it involves unique activities, such as developing linkages among multiple data sets. For all of the activities, Riedel demonstrates that the skills and knowledge required to accomplish them are no less rigorous than the similar skills and knowledge required to conduct original research.

As the scope and cost of large-scale criminological research have increased, secondary data have become an ever-more important asset for criminological research. The federal government frequently spends the greatest proportion of its research support on data collection and the least on analysis. Large studies can support much more analysis than the principal research team is able to accomplish within their funding period. These data, and other agency data originally collected for record keeping or evaluation, are a public resource. Marc Riedel's book shows how to take maximum advantage of the opportunities inherent in research using secondary data.

—Christopher S. Dunn, Ph.D.
*Director, National Archive of Criminal Justice Data,*
*Ann Arbor, Michigan*

# PREFACE

This is the first book of its kind. While that may imply grander things than exist, nearly all of what is discussed here about secondary data in criminology and criminal justice has been used by crime researchers for years. What this volume attempts to do is to synthesize and organize concepts and practices in a manner that students of crime research will find useful. If the synthesis leads to a clearer understanding and use of secondary data by others in disciplines that study crime, so much the better.

The first chapter sets the stage by examining the conceptual foundations of secondary data. The chapter defines secondary data, discusses their advantages and limitations, the types of secondary data, explores the relationship between primary and secondary data with respect to crime, and, finally, discusses three ways that secondary data can be interpreted.

Because I am interested in writing a book that students will find useful in doing research with secondary data, the next three chapters are oriented toward showing students the availability and diversity of secondary data, providing guidelines for evaluating official statistics and records, and procedures for accessing and using official records. Chapter 2 is a description of sources of secondary data, specifically focusing on the Inter-university Consortium for Political and Social Research and the National Archive of Criminal Justice Data. Most of the data sources described in that chapter can be downloaded from the World Wide Web.

Chapter 3 describes the initial stages of research with secondary data. The importance of literature reviews and the nature of hypotheses are discussed. Most of the chapter discusses guidelines that can be used to evaluate the quality of official records and official statistics.

Chapter 4 is, in many ways, the most unusual chapter. Drawing primarily on personal experience, I try to outline the various stages involved in gaining access to official records, the data collection process, management, and quality control issues. There are two caveats in using this chapter.

First, the chapter is meant to be read selectively: For experienced researchers, it may seem long and overdrawn; for novices, it describes the various problems they may face in using official records. Even for the latter, the usefulness of the content has to be considered against access and use in their particular circumstances.

Second, the latter portions of the chapter discuss management and quality control problems and assume the researcher is using official records with a research grant. While most students are not in that position, I took that perspective to give student users, who are frequently research assistants, an administrative overview. While such a view is not immediately relevant, many research assistants are graduate students who will go on to administer funded research projects.

Chapter 5 discusses methodological issues associated with using secondary data to study crime. There is a discussion of classification, disaggregation, missing data, and linkages among and between data sets.

Given the pervasive nature of legal issues in a litigious society, it behooves crime researchers to understand the legal dimensions of secondary data. Chapter 6 provides an extensive discussion of Freedom of Information Acts and subpoenas.

The final chapter is devoted to speculation, which I hope is informed, about the future of secondary data. There are discussions of the contribution of federal agencies to data archives, the growth of qualified users, and how revolutions in computer technology have made the use of secondary data much easier. There seems little doubt that the emergence of the discipline of criminal justice has made enormous contributions to the number of qualified users.

In the final section, there is a discussion of a concept Barney Glaser suggested in 1963. The "Independent Researcher" that Glaser describes has become a much more realistic possibility with the advances of computer technology and the Internet.

The book is written for upper division and graduate students. Because there is enormous overlap in research methods used with secondary and primary data, I refer the reader to standard research methods texts whenever appropriate. Thus, I recommend that the book be used either in conjunction with an introductory textbook on research methods or in subsequent courses that have an elementary research methods course as a prerequisite. I have kept discussion of statistical techniques to an absolute minimum; hence, a course in elementary statistics would be useful, but not essential.

\* \* \*

I would like to extend my appreciation to a number of people who have contributed in a variety of ways to this book. Mark Small, Institute for Family and Neighborhood Life, Clemson University, lent his lawyerly talents to authoring Chapter 6, "Legal Dimensions of Secondary Data." Mark is also a coauthor of Chapter 2, "Sources of Secondary Data."

Lisa Lindhorst used her copyediting skills to help turn initial drafts into polished final products. Lisa's work has contributed substantially to the quality of the final product. I would also like to thank

Wendy C. Regoeczi, University of Toronto, who provided useful comments on Chapter 5.

Thanks also to Melinda Woker who spent many hours with the page proofs hunting down small errors. I also appreciate the work of Jadelynn Hunter who prepared the subject and author indexes.

Frank Cullen, University of Cincinnati, and one anonymous reviewer provided a large number of very helpful suggestions. I have incorporated most of them and must assume responsibility for not incorporating others. Subsequently, I am sure I will wish that I had incorporated more!

I would be remiss if I did not gratefully acknowledge the criminological insights and research skills I gained at the University of Pennsylvania under the tutelage of Thorsten Sellin and Marvin E. Wolfgang. Both have passed away in recent years, but their lessons of scholarship live on in their students.

Finally, there have been a large number of editors at Sage over the tortured history of this volume who have lent their unfailing support. Blaise Simqu initially signed the book for Sage. Other editors who worked on the book include Frances Borghi and Catherine Rossbach. The editor who has worked the longest and with the most patience on this project has been C. Terry Hendrix, and I am very grateful for his support. Kassie Gavrilis has worked for the past year on this project and is clearly one of Sage's up-and-coming stars.

—Marc Riedel
*St. Maarten, N.A.*

# SECONDARY DATA IN CRIMINOLOGY AND CRIMINAL JUSTICE

People who do research on crime depend heavily on secondary data—defined here as the use of statistical material and information originally gathered for another purpose.[1] Crime researchers[2] use information from the Bureau of the Census, National Crime Victimization Survey (NCVS),[3] National Center for Health Statistics (NCHS),[4] Uniform Crime Reporting (UCR)[5] program, and sample surveys done by other people as secondary data sources. In addition, crime researchers assemble research data sets from the official records of police departments, juvenile and adult courts, detention centers, community treatment agencies, probation and parole offices, and prisons.

In an effort to learn what types of data are used by crime researchers, I did an informal survey of the types of data used by two major journals, *Justice Quarterly* and *Criminology*, for the period 1992 through 1996. The results are given in Table 1.1.

**TABLE 1.1** Types of Data Used in *Justice Quarterly* and *Criminology* Articles: 1992–1996

|  | Number of Articles | Percentage No Data | Percentage Primary Data | Percentage Secondary Data | Percentage Combination |
|---|---|---|---|---|---|
| *Justice Quarterly* | 141 | 14.9 | 39.7 | 29.8 | 15.6 |
| *Criminology* | 131 | 19.2 | 17.6 | 56.2 | 8.5 |

Each article for the 5-year period was classified into four categories, excluding book reviews. "No Data" refers to articles, such as theoretical articles, in which research was cited but there was no indication of analysis or manipulation of data. "Primary Data" means data gathered by the authors using interviews or survey methods. "Secondary Data," defined previously, includes archival data, surveys, official records, and official statistics. "Combination" refers to articles that use a combination of primary and secondary data.

Table 1.1 shows that, among all published articles in the two journals, secondary data are more frequently used in *Criminology* (56.2%) than in *Justice Quarterly* (29.8%). *Justice Quarterly* contributors more frequently used primary data (39.7%) than did contributors to *Criminology* (17.6%).

Excluding the "No Data" category, *Justice Quarterly* articles are more evenly divided between primary data (40.7%) and secondary data (35.0%) sources. By comparison, slightly more than one fifth (21.7%) of *Criminology* contributors used primary data, and more than two thirds (68.9%) used secondary data.

Based on this informal and limited survey, it is clear that secondary data are an important source of information about crime. Minimally, almost a third of the articles published in a leading journal use secondary data. For reasons given in a later section, secondary data will continue to be a prominent source of data for disciplines that study crime.

As scientific disciplines mature, they customize the scientific method for their own uses. While many social sciences share a common methodology, every discipline develops its own configuration and emphases. For example, both psychology and sociology make use of survey methodology and experimental design, but experimental design plays a more central role in psychological research than survey methodology, while the reverse is true in sociology.

Perhaps because criminal justice and criminology are relatively young disciplines, there is little information available about the characteristics, uses, strengths, and limitations of secondary data specific to either field. Books focusing on the topic describe sources of secondary data without much discussion of how they are used (Kiecolt & Nathan, 1985). Until recently, research textbooks were targeted to broader student audiences and the topic of secondary data was given little attention. Recent textbooks have been oriented toward criminology and criminal justice students and devote more space to the topic (Futrell & Roberson, 1988; Hagan, 1993; Maxfield & Babbie, 1998).

The scant literature on criminal justice teaching of secondary data use may be understood by considering how the use of official records is taught: Students learn in an apprenticeship fashion reminiscent of medieval craft education. Crime researchers learn from techniques used by their major professors or principal investigators on grants where they have worked how to approach criminal justice agencies for permission to use their records, how to set up a work schedule that does not conflict with agency activities, construct a research design within the limits of available information, and develop a data collection schedule. Seldom is the time taken to collect in one place the body of knowledge regarding secondary data. The purpose of the present volume is to increase the use of secondary data by providing an approach suited to research inquiries that rely on the statistics and records of criminal justice and social service agencies as a source of research data.

## The Uses of Secondary Data

There are several reasons for the frequent use of secondary data in criminology and criminal justice journals. First, many phenomena of interest to crime researchers are so difficult to observe directly that secondary data are the only practical source of data. As a rule, the more serious the crime, the less frequently it occurs and the less likely it can be observed directly. For example, in 1995, there were only 1,221 murders and non-negligent manslaughters in an Illinois population of 11,830,000 (Federal Bureau of Investigation [FBI], 1996). Given its rarity and generally unannounced occurrence, information about criminal homicides must be gathered as a by-product of the investigation and apprehension of offenders.

This is also true of crimes that are more prevalent than criminal homicides but cannot be observed for other reasons. For example, Harries (1989) found that aggravated assaults ($N = 32,096$) occurred 27 times more frequently than criminal homicide ($N = 1,228$) in Dallas from 1981 through 1985. However, aggravated assaults occur in settings that are not routinely subject to surveillance. Thus, robberies, rapes, as well as crimes like burglaries occur in locations and in ways that reduce the possibility of the offender being identified and apprehended. Assaults also occur in settings that are legally protected from outsiders. Thus, the study of domestic violence must be limited to voluntary reports of violence by the victims or offenders because of the protected privacy of the settings (Gelles & Straus, 1988).

Second, information from victimization surveys is secondary data for economic reasons. Victimization surveys require large and expensive samples and repetitive data collection. The cost of such samples and the accompanying data collection is so large that only organizations with access to the resources of a national government can conduct victimization surveys regularly. After initial analyses are reported, the results are placed in an archive for use by secondary analysts. Indeed, to suggest the use of victimization surveys to replace police reports is merely to suggest a different type of secondary data.

Third, secondary data are often used to evaluate the functioning of criminal justice agencies. This kind of research can take two forms. One approach views agency statistics and records as objective indicators of organizational effectiveness. Thus, a higher percentage of arrest clearances for homicide in one police department in comparison to another may be used to show that the former provides more effective law enforcement services, although such a conclusion should be stated with caution (Riedel & Jarvis, 1998).

A second form of evaluation views agency statistics and records as indicators of organizational processes. Official statistics are not viewed as accurate indicators of crime, but as representations of individual and institutional policies and practices (Biderman & Reiss, 1967; Kitsuse & Cicourel, 1963). Arrests for illegal gambling, for example, represent police responses to public pressures to do something about crime more than they represent an indication of the actual incidence.

Fourth, secondary data are a major source of information in cross-cultural or transnational research. Most cross-cultural research relies on United Nations surveys, World Health Organization, and International Police Organization (INTERPOL) statistics drawn from police and medical records of various countries (Gartner, 1997). The Comparative Crime Data File assembled by Archer and Gartner (1984) has crime data from 110 countries and 44 cities for 1900 through 1970. Such a file would be impossible to assemble without using official statistics and records from other countries.

Fifth, secondary data are important sources of data for assessing changes occurring at the same time in different places. For example, research by Riedel, Zahn, and Mock (1985) compared patterns of homicides in eight different cities for one year (1978).

Secondary data can be used to assess changes at different times in the same place. Because information is collected and organized by agencies over a long period, it can be used to examine crime trends. Using data from Statistics Canada, Silverman and Kennedy (1987) examined trends in homicide victim-offender relationships for 1961 through 1983. Trend studies based on secondary data can form the basis for evaluating the effect of a change in legislation or policy. For example, Campbell and Ross's (1980) frequently cited evaluation of a crackdown on speeding in Connecticut compared traffic fatalities in that state to comparable data in other states for a nine-year period.

The records of agencies are also a useful source of data for another type of longitudinal design, studying careers in crime. For example, Wolfgang, Figlio, and Sellin (1972) constructed a cohort and examined the delinquency involvement of males born in 1945 who resided in Philadelphia from age 10 to 18 by using school and police records. Records of agencies, along with other types of data, are being used in the current Harvard Project on Human Development, an 8-year study under way to uncover correlates of criminality over the life span *(http://phdcn.harvard.edu/geninfo.htm)*.

Sixth, secondary data are useful for replication. Replication is different from repetition or duplication; the word derives from *replicare*, which means "to reply." In this instance, the researcher is replying or responding to the original research by raising questions about the reproducibility or generalizability of the original results. In addition, by logically consistent inferences, the replicated study can generate new and unexpected consequences (Finifter, 1975).

For example, Sherman and Berk (1984) completed a landmark study of domestic violence in Minneapolis in which they found that arrest was more effective in reducing domestic violence than counseling both parties or sending assailants away. Because police data on domestic violence are available in other cities, this study led to replications in six other jurisdictions. These replications did not support the finding that arrest is an effective deterrent to spousal assault. Paternoster, Brame, Bachman, and Sherman (1997) subsequently reanalyzed data from one of the sites, Milwaukee, and concluded that how the offender was treated—procedural justice—was as important as arrest in explaining changes in spousal assault.

Finally, secondary data are important because they are accessible and inexpensive. As funds for research become scarce, sources of information that require less money, less time, and fewer personnel become more attractive. Because the necessity for understanding the causes and consequences of crime continue, the demand for research production, especially in academia, remains the same or is increasing.

Secondary data are a valuable source to researchers who have limited money and time for research. Because data collection is the most expensive and time-consuming part of research, secondary data are especially important to dissertation students and faculty in colleges where the major activity is teaching (Glaser, 1963).

Secondary data are readily accessible to researchers. Several of the largest data archives in the world are located in the United States. According to Kiecolt and Nathan (1985), the largest data archive is the Inter-university Consortium of Political and Social Research (ICPSR) at the University of Michigan. This archive holds data from more than 1,700 studies divided into about 26,000 machine-readable files covering approximately 130 countries. Of those, more than 500 are crime-related studies. Examples of these data sets and more detailed descriptions are provided in Chapter 2.

## Disadvantages of Secondary Data

Perhaps the major disadvantage of secondary data is that indicators needed for the proposed research are not readily available among secondary data sets. Because the fit between indicator and concept is not as close as could be achieved with primary data, the secondary user is faced with the persistent problem of the validity of the relation between the old indicator and the new concept (Hyman, 1972). In other words, the data available may not answer the question posed.

Unfortunately, there is no simple solution to the problem. Crime researchers have to call upon their creative abilities to refashion tools that were originally meant to serve other purposes. Where it is not possible to find an indicator that represents a good fit with the concept, it is possible to use several weak indicators and explore their adequacy as measures by additional analysis.

In addition, secondary data may be aggregated at a level that cannot be used to answer questions. For example, the UCR aggregates arrests monthly by the age, ethnic origin, and gender of the arrestees. For research designs that demand comparisons between multidimensional categories of individuals (young black males vs. young white males), the data cannot be used.

Another problem is that codes and operational definitions may be inadequately specified. For example, before 1980, the Supplementary Homicide Reports (SHR)[6] used the following codes for race of victim and offender: White, Negro, Indian, Chinese, Japanese, Other, Unknown. While this classification may reflect the frequency of involvement in crime of racial or ethnic groups, it is difficult to compare categories from the SHR with racial or ethnic classifications used more generally. It is unclear why a classification by major racial groups, implemented in 1980, was not used previously (Riedel, 1990, 1999).

A related problem occurs in some agency records where different operational definitions of the variables occur over time as those responsible for inputting data change. For secondary data on crime, the problem of inadequate documentation is more pronounced for official or agency records versus official statistics such as the UCR. Indeed, as will be discussed later, a major problem with using official records is that the crime researcher must create the documentation from information available in the files.

Another major disadvantage of secondary data on crime is missing information. The number of unrecorded crimes, or "dark number," not only refers to crimes that go unreported by victims and community members, but also to the problems of recording that are the result of organizational policies and practices. These issues will be discussed in greater detail in Chapter 5.

## Types of Secondary Data

There are three major types of secondary data discussed in this book: surveys, official statistics, and official records. Depending on how the data are stored, each may also be referred to as archival data. In the past, a major problem facing secondary data users was determining the availability of the data set, its quality, and documentation (Hyman, 1972). The emergence of archives did not, per se, lead to better data, but archival description, classification, and documentation does allow the secondary data user to review and compare the characteristics of a large variety of data sets in detail (see Chapter 2).

Surveys are characterized by data acquired through questionnaires or interviews and, generally, probability sampling. The best-known are the NCVS; the National Youth Survey, which is a 5-year panel study using self-report techniques of a national probability sample of 1,726 persons age 11 to 17 in 1976 (Elliott & Ageton, 1980); and the Survey of Inmates of Adult Correctional Facilities administered by the Bureau of Justice Statistics (Baunach, 1990).

Official statistics and official records[7] are collections of information maintained and made available in permanent form by organizations that frequently retain a proprietary interest in their use. The best-known official statistics are the Uniform Crime Reports. The National Archive of Criminal Justice Data *(http://www.icpsr.umich. edu/NACJD/)* stores data sets from a variety of criminal justice agencies: National Institute of Justice, Bureau of Justice Statistics, U.S. Sentencing Commission, Pretrial Services Resource Center, and the Bureau of Prisons. Archived data will be discussed in the next chapter.

Official records are collections of statistical data that are generated as an organizational by-product of another mission or goal. Examples of official records include information from a variety of criminal justice agencies such as police departments, treatment agencies, probation departments, and the like.

There are several differences between official statistics and official records. First, because official records are gathered as a by-product of other activity, they are not designed or maintained for public consumption or research use. By contrast, official statistics are presented in formats that are more easily used by researchers.

Second, because official records were constructed for internal use, they are more difficult to access for research use compared to official statistics. Official statistics are frequently freely available through either parent agencies or archives.

Third, for each record, the amount of detail is typically greater for official records than for official statistics. Because official statistics are collected from many agencies and are meant to be disseminated widely, they focus on a few data elements that are typically reported accurately and consistently.

Fourth, for official records, the data are usually based on a unit of analysis that is the same as the target of the service delivery effort, usually a person. Thus, police collect data on victims and suspects, and courts collect data on defendants. Official statistics, on the other hand, may be available only at higher levels of aggregation such as monthly arrests or convictions.

Finally, Hakim (1983) has noted that in the collection of information from official records, recorders, the persons who originally complete the forms, may be present in the agency and accessible to the researcher. This gives the researcher an opportunity to learn more about how the information is gathered. Official statistics, on the other hand, are gathered from many different agencies. Although recorders typically are not available, procedures followed usually are available.

## The Meanings of Secondary Data

Any research problem or hypothesis using secondary data includes presuppositions about the nature of the data. For example, crime researchers who use police records to study patterns of homicide may assume that these files contain information on the vast majority of legally defined acts of killing. By contrast, crime researchers are sufficiently knowledgeable about the reporting of prostitution that they would not assume police records reflect the amount of legally defined prostitution. Rather, crime researchers would view prostitution arrests as indicators of variations in police activity that, in turn, is a response to public and media pressure to "do something" about vice. While there are some variations and overlap, most of the interpretations of official statistics and records can be grouped into three categories: positivist-realist, institutionalist, and radical (Biderman & Reiss, 1967; Jupp, 1989).

Drawing largely from early positivism and influenced by Durkheim's (1951) study of suicide, the realist position views secondary data on crime as *objective indicators* of a phenomenon. In this view, the number of murders and non-negligent manslaughters reported by the UCR actually represents the vast majority of intentional killings in the United States.

Crime researchers may treat secondary data as objective indicators, but they do not do so uncritically. The view of official statistics and records as rough approximations of the "true" level of crime calls for methodological and technical devices to compensate for shortcomings in the data. Victim surveys, self-report studies, and estimation techniques for missing data are used to strengthen inferences based on secondary data.

In contrast to the realist view that "there exists an external, objective 'crime reality' waiting to be discovered" (Bottomley, 1979, p. 23), the institutionalists hold that crime statistics are *products* of the criminal justice system and the activities of the people who work in it. "In this sense, official statistics are not more or less accurate measures of crime upon which to base causal explanations, but representation of individual and institutional polices and practices" (Jupp, 1989, p. 93). In this view, the focus of the inquiry is what the secondary data represent with respect to their production rather than what they represent with respect to the phenomena they purport to measure (Jupp, 1989; Kitsuse & Cicourel, 1963).

In his study of juvenile justice, Cicourel (1968) notes that the view of official data as objective indicators obscures the view that official statistics reflect socially organized activities divorced from the sociological theories used retrospectively for explaining the same statistics. Members of the community, law enforcement personnel, attorneys, judges, all respond to various behavioral or imputed symbolic or reported acts and events by juveniles with commonsense or lay conceptions, abstract legal rules, bureaucratic procedures and policies. (p. 37)

But there is a difficulty in viewing official statistics and records solely as products, as Jupp (1989) has noted. By rejecting official statistics and focusing on the interaction of individuals and representatives of the criminal justice system in particular circumstances, there is a danger of limiting explanation to the dynamics of those interactions. While police are given a measure of discretion in deciding whether an act should be treated as a crime, the meanings and definitions attributed to the behavior are constrained, but not determined, by a role that is part of a criminal justice organization with its own policies and practices.

The institutionalist perspective developed by Bottomley (1979) and his colleagues (Bottomley & Coleman, 1981; Bottomley & Pease, 1986) takes Jupp's concerns into account. Bottomley and Coleman (1981) view official statistics and records as the product of a social process dependent on the social definitions and interactions of offenders, members of the community (victims, witnesses), and representatives of the criminal justice system. Thus, actions by the various parties that might lead to biased or unreliable statistics from the realist view are taken in the institutionalist view to be part of the sociological reality that gives meaning to the official statistics.

In this interpretation, acts brought to the attention of police are those about which victims or community members believe something should be done. The various levels of official statistics, such as police and judicial, are seen as "gates" with counting mechanisms. Thus, official statistics can be characterized not only in terms of their accuracy, but also with respect to different purposes that can be employed validly at each level. Rather than a wholesale rejection or acceptance of official statistics and records, the crime researcher is put in the position of examining specific data sets for both their accuracy and the purposes they might validly serve.

The radical interpretation treats official statistics as *symptoms:* Official information is seen as a reflection of the structure of society, particularly class relations, and how the latter structural features affect the generation of crime and crime statistics (Jupp, 1989). In the closing chapter of a radical critique of official statistics, Griffiths, Irvine, and Miles (1979) note that

> close inspection reveals that arguments for the objectivity and rationality of statistics cloak a social framework of control and exploitation, which itself conditions the development and application of statistical data and methods. Thus, for example, the section of this book which assessed official statistics demonstrated that these data are preconceptualized and produced according to the ideology of the ruling class, and its interests, articulated and co-ordinated through the state. (p. 364)

There is little doubt that treating official statistics and records as "symptoms" of a capitalist order has made a positive contribution. First, the concern with patterns of law enforcement points the way to a consideration of the economically powerful whose crimes are under-represented in official information. Second, the focus on official statistics and records as an organizational product places the burden of explanation on the small-scale interactions that occur in criminal justice organizations. Yet organizations do not exist in a vacuum. While organizational processes do explain how crime data are produced, practices and policies also reflect the inter-connection of organizations with broader social structural forces. Third, the radical view of official statistics and records has the virtue of "dragging the state centre stage" and provoking questions about how statistics are used (Jupp, 1989, p. 100). It is the power of the state that sanctions acts it designates as crimes, and a perspective that keeps that fact at the forefront makes an important contribution.

Treating official statistics and records as symptoms does, however, have its difficulties. The use of the term *symptom* implies that there is an underlying reality that accounts for the statistics. But whose reality? An extreme view suggests that official statistics and records can be viewed only through the subjective experiences of police officers and the assumptions of crime researchers. Under such circumstances, rational knowledge is difficult, if not impossible.

Bulmer (1984) seems to have summarized the difficulties:

> The most difficult questions arise, of course, in the *inter-play between* categories and evidence, between concepts and empirical data. It is here that sociologists have in principle much to contribute to the work of official statisticians. . . . Unfortunately, this potential sociological contribution to social statistics is all too easily sidetracked by either over-determinist claims for the theory-laden status of sociological knowledge, or over-simple political analyses which purport to show that "official statistics" form part of the process of maintaining and reproducing the dominant ideologies of capitalist society. . . . Would that it were all so straightforward and reducible to the right political analysis and allegiance! (italics in the original; pp. 144-145)

General categories, Bulmer suggests, pose autonomous scientific problems that do not support one point of view. Consider the body of research on the death penalty. Much of the research that has consistently demonstrated racial discrimination in the imposition of the death penalty has come from official statistics or official records (Baldus, Pulaski, & Woodworth, 1983, 1986; Bowers & Pierce, 1980; Gross & Mauro, 1984; Radelet, 1981; Riedel, 1976; Wolfgang & Riedel, 1973). Rather than supporting capitalist ideology, that body of research has consistently shown that the death penalty is legally arbitrary, hardly a conclusion that would strengthen elements in the judiciary interested in class exploitation.

Which interpretation of secondary data on crime is taken is determined not so much by the statistics as by the theoretical positions that cluster around the realist, institutionalist, and radical interpretations. There is not a single question to be asked of such numbers; there are many. The challenge for crime researchers is to understand how official records and statistics are originally collected and to incorporate this knowledge into their assessment of its use and quality, the construction of hypotheses, research designs, and interpretation of the results.

## Secondary Data in Social Science

The distinction between primary and secondary data is traditionally associated with historical research (Ritter, 1986). Gustavson (1955) states that primary sources are accounts by eyewitnesses or contemporaries of the events. Abraham Lincoln is dead and the next best source of what he thought is letters or accounts by people who knew him. By contrast, secondary sources are historical accounts written by persons who have studied primary sources. A contemporary view is that the validity of the data source, that is, the most accurate representation of a past event, is more important than what is included in the categories of original and derived evidence (Barzun & Graff, 1985).

The distinction between primary and secondary data is different for crime researchers. The use of secondary data means that direct observation is neither practical nor appropriate. It may not be realistic or practical to observe homicides in any number, but, unlike past events, it is possible. Likewise, direct observation may not be appropriate where secondary data are used to measure agency functioning, for example. This, of course, does not preclude the use of primary data where easily available. While secondary data can be used to study homicides, primary data can also be used where offenders, survivors, and bystanders are interviewed.

In this perspective, the view that the distinction between primary and secondary data is a distinction between official records and official statistics is a misconception. The view is that researchers who go to police departments to collect data from their records, for example, are using primary data. The verb *collect* means to gather or bring together in one body or place; the mere act of gathering data from an agency does not qualify the data as primary, since both primary and secondary data can be "collected." Thus, information collected from police records is secondary data because police records were originally information collected for another purpose.

## Secondary Data on Crime

At least for official records and official statistics, secondary data on crime share with other social science secondary data the characteristic that data are organizational definitions of events. Rather than the "definition of events" imposed by researchers who design questionnaires or interviews, secondary data begin with a selection and description of events by criminal justice and other agencies who originally collected the data. In that sense, homicide is generally what police, courts, judges, and juries say it is.

Economics is a discipline that depends on organizational definitions of events in the form of official statistics. As Hyman (1972) notes, "The economists have been *secondary* analysts for many years, living off the long time series on prices, employment, population, etc. produced by the government" (italics in the original; p. 215).

Emphasizing that secondary data, in contrast to primary data, depend on organizational definitions of events does not mean the data are less valid or reliable. However, it does suggest that users have to take into account how the event is defined by the original collectors, the counting rules, and how consistently they are applied.

Further, the repeated use of official statistics, regardless of field of study, benefits disciplines because the use of the same data sets means that inferences from the data are reviewed by others. The robustness of variables is checked by different methods of analysis and the addition of other variables.

Finally, the use of secondary data sources pays dividends to data sources as well. The detailed use of data by researchers reveals the strengths and limitations in ways that are not always apparent to the organizational users. Such information can be used by data sources to improve the quality of data collection systems. For example, compared to UCR, NCHS has a long history of cooperation with researchers. As a result, the strengths and limitations of homicide data from mortality statistics are better known than similar data from UCR (Riedel, 1990).

## Is Secondary Data on Crime Different?

Secondary data on crime may also be different from other types of social science secondary data. Discussions of secondary data have been most directly influenced through sociology and the analysis of secondary data. One of the first efforts to describe the principles of secondary data focused on secondary analysis of social surveys. Hyman's (1972) seminal volume described how previous surveys and survey items can be taken apart and combined in new ways to study social groups, change, and make cross-national comparisons.

However, the issues relating to the analysis of surveys miss a critical issue for crime researchers. Writing on secondary data has focused on secondary *analysis,* that is, problems related to the use of sample surveys (Hyman, 1972; Jacob, 1984). While the latter have been substantial contributions, the approach leaves a gap in the crime literature. By focusing on secondary *analysis* rather than secondary *data,* problems related to assembling data sets from the official records of criminal justice agencies are ignored. Issues of analyses that occur *after* the data sets have been assembled are very different from those that involve access, data collection, and use of official statistics and records.

British sociologists have paid more attention to the use of official statistics and records than their counterparts in the United States. The greater attention extends beyond useful guides to data sources and examples (Hakim, 1982b) and how to access and use government surveys (Dale, Arber, & Procter, 1988). What are most useful are discussions of conceptual and theoretical issues related to the use of official statistics (Bulmer, 1984; Hindess, 1973; Irvine, Miles, & Evans, 1979), research designs (Hakim, 1987), research methods (Jupp, 1989), the use of official records (Hakim, 1983), and relationships between official and academic social research (Hakim, 1982a).

British writers on the general topic of secondary data acknowledge that crime-related secondary data are different—and worse. For example, Bulmer (1984) notes that the "special problems of reliable and valid measurement" in official statistics of crime and delinquency are "notorious" (p. 135). Similarly, in comparing types of official records, Hakim (1987) notes "a conventional view that data from administrative records is seriously deficient, particularly in relation to value-laden topics such as crime" (p. 42). Within the United States, it is worth noting that Hyman (1972), who enthusiastically endorsed secondary analyses of surveys, makes no mention of well-known victimization surveys that were surely available (Ennis, 1967).

One major difference between crime and non-crime secondary data revolves around *content*. There is a fundamental difference between systems that record routine behavior and note the exceptional and those that record exceptional behavior and note the routine. There are many record systems that report widely shared characteristics. Attitudes about a variety of social issues, and official statistics about education, health, employment, and political behavior are examples. The thrust of the analysis focuses on the entire range of variation that is found in the data.

On the other hand, consider the NCVS. In order to locate a sufficiently large number of crime victimizations, interviews have to be conducted with an extremely large number of people, many of whom report no victimizations. The NCVS conducts interviews each year with approximately 43,000 households and 80,000 people age 12 and older. Out of this number, 34,788 reported victimizations are the focus of analysis (Bureau of Justice Statistics [BJS], 1998). While there are some comparisons to those who report no victimization, an important part of the analysis focuses on variation within the sub-group of victims.

In large part, crime is exceptional behavior because it is an emotionally charged event. A major reason for the amount of unreported crime is the seriousness of the event. In the NCVS, the respondent is asked whether he or she reported the victimization to the police. Of violent crimes, aggravated assaults, 59% were reported to the police, but only 28% of thefts (BJS, 1998).

Victims have a clear interest in reporting crimes because they seek justice, retribution, and/or restitution for an injury suffered. However, crimes may go unreported because victims are legally implicated in the offense. This is the case for prostitution, gambling, and drug offenses. Aside from legal accountability, victims may not report crime because they fear humiliation, embarrassment, or offenders. For this reason, spousal and child abuse, sexual assaults, and rapes are under-reported.

Because crime is stigmatizing and carries with it penal sanctions, large portions of the record may be missing, even though the crime is reported. Obviously, offenders have the greatest interest in concealing events. Except for that supplied by the victim, information about the offender depends upon clearing an offense by the arrest of one or more offenders. Clearance percentages are very low; the clearance percentage for the most serious crime, homicide, was 64.8% in 1995 (FBI, 1996). This means that official statistics and records are missing information about an important participant in the crime for more than one third of these cases.

In addition to crimes being emotionally charged events, they are also rare or unusual events. Excited and unaccustomed to such behavior, victims and witnesses provide descriptions that vary according to their concerns and constraints. They are, for example, frequently unable to distinguish between what is a crime according to the police and what is not. They may be unable to distinguish between criminal or civil conflicts (Reiss, 1971). Victims, who may be unwilling to report violence at the hands of family members and friends, may attempt to "normalize" it by treating it as a private matter (Black, 1970).

Victims may respond differently depending on what is considered "normal" in their particular environments. For example, victimization surveys find that victimization by assault is positively correlated with education despite the fact that police files indicate that most victims of assault are lower class. It may be that better-educated persons are better respondents and give more information. However, it is also likely that lower-class persons may see certain types of violence as a normal part of life, whereas better-educated persons have had very little contact with physically assaultive behavior and see such acts as criminal violence (Skogan, 1981).

The nature of the event also has an impact on those charged with investigating, effecting arrests, and gathering information. Because it is not known when and where crimes occur, information collection is costly. This limits data sets to collection efforts that have the resources of a government or to information that is collected as a by-product of some other socially important activity, such as law enforcement. Unlike surveys of prevalent characteristics or behavior, which can be conducted frequently and inexpensively, reports of crime rely heavily on relatively few sources.

Police officers investigating a crime make an effort to be responsive to demands of an emotionally charged situation while also trying to gathering requisite information to determine that a crime has occurred. Organizational and occupational factors influence police reporting decisions, but not always in a way that is contrary to victim perceptions of the event. The more serious the crime, the more likely the police are to report it, and citizens and police use very similar criteria of "seriousness." Further, police rarely report a crime if victims prefer to treat the matter informally (Gove, Hughes, & Geerken, 1985).

Police reporting is affected by other aspects of the situation. Police are more likely to report the crime if the complainant is deferential, a bystander is present, and the suspect is a stranger (O'Brien, 1985).

The reporting of crime is also influenced by characteristics of police organizations, policies set internally by police organizations, and those imposed from the outside. For example, more professional police departments report more crime (Skogan, 1976).

Finally, internal changes in police departments and prosecuting attorney's offices have an impact on crime reporting. Policy directives ordering more thorough investigation of certain crimes and changes in supervisory police personnel, such as commanders or sergeants, have been shown to have an impact on how much crime is reported (O'Brien, 1985).

Given the nature of crime as an exceptional event and problems involved in its collection, it is no surprise that crime data have not been viewed with enthusiasm by users of secondary data about routine events. More so than with other kinds of data, there is no way of "objectively" identifying crime independently of the systems used to count it. The layers of meaning added by an excited victim, an absent offender, and police who are trying to balance public concerns with legal and organizational responsibilities give secondary data on crime a distinctive character.

There are two general implications to be drawn from the preceding discussion. First, if there are no objective ways of observing crimes that are independent of the counting systems used, different data sources have to be evaluated in terms of their strengths and weaknesses vis-à-vis other counting systems. Arguments about the general validity of one secondary data source over another are futile. As Biderman and Lynch (1991) have noted, differences between levels of crime reported in the UCR and in the National Crime Survey are, in many cases, the result of differences in procedures.

Second, the essential character of crime is not likely to change. However, crime researchers have worked diligently to improve on existing methods of collecting crime data and to develop alternative approaches. This not only includes various techniques of direct observation, but also self-reports and victimization surveys. Because different methods and procedures are intricately inter-woven with reports on crime, the secondary data user is required to be intimately familiar with the full range of methods and procedures so as to determine the suitability of the data for testing hypotheses and examining research problems.

## Conclusions

This chapter has tried to organize and synthesize existing conceptual material on secondary data in an effort to forge an approach useful in crime research. Secondary data have been defined as information gathered for some other purpose. The remainder of the book will focus on quantitative data, with a heavy emphasis on official records and official statistics because that seems to be a prominent feature of crime research. There is no implication in the latter that qualitative secondary data are superior to the quantitative kind or that researchers should not use primary data whenever feasible.

What is important to the disciplines that study crime is the development of a methodological approach to secondary data. Disciplines that study crime are sufficiently mature to "customize" the scientific method for their own purposes.

In organizing and synthesizing material, a number of tasks have been attempted. Four types of secondary data (surveys, official records, official statistics, and archival data) have been described and their similarities and differences discussed.

It has been shown that official records and official statistics can be interpreted in different ways depending on the purpose of the inquiry. Secondary data can be viewed as objective indicators of a phenomenon, products of organizational activity, or symptoms of an underlying reality.

Finally, there has been an effort to address the question of primary and secondary data in relation to other disciplines. It was suggested that official statistics and records on crime are organizational definitions of events. If that is the case, it behooves crime researchers to be aware of the context of data collection. What may well distinguish secondary data on crime from secondary data in other disciplines is the nature of the phenomenon: collecting information on crime is not like collecting data on consumer purchases, for example.

Rather than lamenting the woes of crime data, the layers of meaning contributed by reporters and recorders are part of the problem. While the meanings of crime data are several, it seems that secondary data are most nearly described by Bottomley and his colleagues as "gates" with counting mechanisms; that view is built upon in subsequent chapters.

Chapter 2 describes sources of secondary data. There is an examination of the different federal agencies and the kind of data available from each agency. Chapter 2 also discusses the enormous variety of data sets available from the Inter-university Consortium for Political and Social Research. Finally, because some data sets are so large that downloading them is a practical impossibility, there is an examination of emerging methods for building data sets on-line.

Chapter 3 and Chapter 4 are designed to be practical sources of information for people who have limited experience with secondary data. In Chapter 3, a large number of guidelines is given for evaluating a secondary data set. In Chapter 4, the different phases of accessing and using official records are described, ranging from initial contacts to the process of data collection.

Chapter 5 is a consideration of methodological issues. This chapter examines classification and the problems associated with disaggregating data, missing data, and linkages within and between data sets.

Chapter 6 is given over to a discussion of the legal dimensions of secondary data. Because most crime researchers are unaware of the legal issues created by the use of secondary data, two legal issues are discussed: freedom of information acts and subpoenas.

The final chapter discusses the future of secondary data. There is a discussion of how the emergence of criminal justice as a discipline has contributed to the increased use of secondary data. Perhaps most impressive and unpredictable is the emergence of computing technology and the Internet that will revolutionize the use of secondary data. Perhaps the most intriguing idea is the use of archival data, the Internet, and powerful personal computers in the hands of what Barney Glaser in 1963 called the "independent researcher."

## Notes

1. This definition is borrowed from Stewart (1984): "the use of . . . statistical material and information not specifically gathered for the research question at hand" (p. 11). The definition used here does differ from those that define secondary data as data gathered by other *people* (Jupp, 1989, p. 11) or individuals *who were not part of the original research team* (Traugott, 1990, p. 145).

What is critical is that the original data are being used for a different *purpose*. It does not matter whether the person who originally collected the data now proposes to use them as secondary data. Although Hyman (1972) has suggested that the original collector of the information may be more knowledgeable and have easier access to the data set than the ordinary secondary data user, other major issues and problems surrounding its use remain the same for both types of users.

Purpose is expressed when a secondary analyst "by an act of *abstraction* uses questions originally employed to indicate one entity to illuminate other aspects that a former analyst did not have in mind at all" (italics in the original; Hyman, 1972, p. 37).

2. Rather than using the cumbersome phrase "criminological and criminal justice researchers" throughout the book, a generic role descriptor, "crime researchers," refers to persons from a variety of disciplines who use empirical research methods to study crime. For similar reasons of economy, generic descriptors such as "agency administrators" or "recorders" are used in subsequent chapters. In each case, a definition of the major activities of the holder of the roles is provided.

3. The National Crime Victimization Survey (NCVS) is a continuing survey of a national probability sample. Interviews are conducted with a member(s) of each household in the sample to determine the extent and patterns of criminal victimization. For a more detailed discussion, see Garofalo (1990) and Biderman and Lynch (1991).

4. Homicide data from the Vital Statistics Division of the National Center for Health Statistics are part of a nationwide collection of mortality data. Homicide data are collected using a standardized death certificate, which includes information on the cause of death, age, race, gender, and place of residence of the victim, and place of incident's occurrence. For a detailed description, see Riedel (1999).

5. The Uniform Crime Reporting program is the oldest continuing series for recording crimes known to the police in the United States. The program is administered by the Federal Bureau of Investigation and depends on monthly reports from police departments. The UCR program collects data on five general reporting forms: crimes known to the police; property stolen and recovered; supplementary homicide reports; age, sex, race, and ethnic origin of person arrested; and infor-

mation on police employees. For a discussion of the program, see Schneider and Wiersema (1990) and Biderman and Lynch (1991).

6. The Supplementary Homicide Reports are part of the UCR program (see Note 5). Unlike other UCR forms that aggregate data, the SHR is based on the homicide event. It includes information on the age, ethnic origin, and gender of the victim and offender; circumstances; victim-offender relationship; and weapon. For a description, see Riedel (1990, 1999).

7. In referring to the statistics or records of an organization as "official," there may be a risk of connotatively conferring more authority or legitimacy on them than intended. As used here, *official* means the records or statistics of an office. This use is similar to Weber's (1946a) characterization of the management of a modern bureaucratic office as based on written documents (the files).

# 2

# SOURCES OF SECONDARY DATA

A description of the large amount of archived data in the United States is a book in itself. Indeed, for a general review of the large number of secondary data sources, the reader is advised to consult Kiecolt and Nathan (1985).

There is little doubt that the major source of crime-related secondary data is the Inter-university Consortium for Political and Social Research (ICPSR) located at the Institute for Social Research, University of Michigan, Ann Arbor. While much of the chapter will focus on secondary data sets available from ICPSR and the National Archive of Criminal Justice Data (NACJD), other secondary data sources are also described.

Most of the references to data sources will give an Internet address for two reasons. First, for many data sets, the Internet address is also either the site for downloading data or contains a link to the data archive. Second, the nature of archives changes constantly as data sets are added, modified, or removed. Likewise, policies, practices, and Internet locations change so rapidly that conventionally published material quickly becomes dated. For those who require the additional information, the addresses for data archives described in the text are given in the Appendix.

The present chapter is divided into four parts. In the first part, general holdings of ICPSR relevant to crime are discussed. The second part focuses on NACJD, which is part of ICPSR. Because many of the data sets are the result of research sponsored by federal agencies, holdings sponsored by two major criminal justice agencies, the National Institute of Justice and the Bureau of Justice Statistics, are described. The third section describes other sources of secondary data.

The final section describes how subsets of data can be constructed on-line and downloaded for analysis. Because some data sets are so large that downloading the entire data set is impracticable, the alternative is to construct data sets on-line.

## The Inter-University Consortium for Political and Social Research (ICPSR)

The single best and most current source of information about ICPSR is their home page on the World Wide Web (*http://www.icpsr.umich. edu/index.html*). This site describes the structure and functioning of the consortium, available publications, summer programs, and the available data sets. As of July 1999, there were 4,500 study titles in the ICPSR archive, comprising more than 40,000 files. There are currently 670 study titles in the NACJD archive.

The following is a description of specific data sources related to criminal justice and criminology available through ICPSR. Virtually all requests for information that come from one of the 325 member institutions are provided to the researcher without cost, while analogous services are provided on a charge basis to individuals who are not so affiliated. The following section summarizes crime-related archival holdings and desktop holdings.

## Crime-Related Archival Holdings

There is a directory of thousands of data sets available in the archives of ICPSR. These data sets are organized into sub-headings and available in machine-readable form. The following is a list of the sub-headings with selected data sets appropriate for crime research. Examples of available data sets pertinent to crime research within each list are provided. The idea behind giving examples from each sub-category is not only to demonstrate the diversity of data available, but also to reveal how seemingly disparate databases might have implications for crime research.

### *Census Enumerations: Historical and Contemporary Population Characteristics*

The most frequently utilized and well-known data sets within this category are the surveys conducted every decade by the Bureau of the Census. The earliest data set available is the 1850 and 1860 Population of Counties, Towns, and Cities in the United States. For those interested in bringing a historical perspective to their work, specific variables include tabulations of white, black, and slave males and females, and aggregate populations for each town.

The most recent data sets available are from the 1990 census. The 1990 census contains an enormous amount of data that have been sorted into various data sets. For example, in one data set derived from the 1990 census of population and housing, race and age are tabulated by sex and Hispanic origin for several layers of geography. Interestingly, almost 10 million respondents checked "other race" and were not included in one of the 15 racial categories offered in the census survey. This finding alone demonstrates the difficulty of using racial categories (e.g., "black, white, other") in research without some qualifying discussion.

The data available from the Census surveys provide an excellent source of information for context and to make comparisons. Because the level of information available is so detailed, comparisons are possible at a local level.

### Conflict, Aggression, Violence, Wars

Because most of the data sources within this area focus on conflict and stability within countries, the data sets would be of interest to those with an international focus to their research. For example, there is one specific database dealing with assassinations, either plotted, attempted, or actual murders of prominent public figures. For each event, information is presented on the country, date and location of occurrence, the actual name of the assassin and of the target, the issue, the type of group to which the assassin belonged, and the political position of the target. The data were gathered from the *The New York Times Index*, from 84 countries and cover the period 1948 through 1967.

### Economic Behavior and Attitudes

Although databases on economic behavior and attitudes might seem unusual for those interested in crime research, a number of data sources provide pertinent contextual information for those interested in relating economic and crime variables. Annual surveys of consumer attitudes and behavior, and surveys of consumer finances and of consumer expenditures all provide useful background information for those interested in property crimes, business crimes, or white-collar offenses.

### Education

There are a few databases in education that appear directly relevant to the study of crime and criminal justice. Perhaps of most relevance is the Safe School Study, a database collected by the Research Triangle Institute and sponsored by the National Institute of Education. The 1976-1977 data were obtained from approximately 30,000 students, 24,000 teachers, and 15,000 principals to ascertain the nature and extent of crimes in schools. Also within this category of research data are a variety of databases collected by the National Center for Education Statistics that cover characteristics of various educational institutions.

### Governmental Structures, Policies, and Capabilities

Within this category, an interesting data set titled "Decision-Related Research on the Organization of Service Delivery Systems in Metropolitan Areas: Police Protection" is available. The project investigated the delivery of police services. The research design included five major clusters of variables: service conditions, the legal structure, organizational arrangements, manpower levels, and expenditure levels. Data were collected in a sample of 80 standard metropolitan statistical areas relating to patrol, criminal investigation, and adult pre-trial detention.

### Health Care and Health Facilities

The majority of data found in health care and health facility databases are polls of various populations querying about health-related attitudes and behaviors. Thus, the majority of data are based on self-report. While some seemingly obscure databases exist (e.g., "Height and Weight of West Point Cadets, 1843-1894"), there are a number of others that involve health-related data that are frequently discussed in crime research. For example, for a number of years a National Health Survey has been conducted that assesses attitudes and knowledge about a wide range of health topics. More recent supplements to this survey have targeted populations' specific knowledge and attitudes toward AIDS and drug and alcohol use.

### Instructional Packages and Computer Programs

Along with databases, ICPSR also contains some instructional packages. Most of the instructional packages and computer programs within this area are related to voting behavior and political science, but a few could be used by instructors in criminology/criminal justice courses. There is a "Domestic Violence Teaching Package, 1955-1964," available to examine current theories of domestic violence, and it is supplemented by a manual, "Workbook for the Analysis of Domestic Violence."

### Legal Systems

Databases on both civil and criminal aspects of the legal system are available for secondary analysis. "Access to Justice in Ontario, 1985-1988" is a good example of research that crosses both legal systems. Respondents were asked about the nature of criminal justice-related problems their households had experienced. Questions were also asked about actions taken in response to the problem, such as whether non-lawyer assistance was sought, whether a claim was made, and reasons for not making a claim. A probability sample was selected using random digit dialing.

Other databases include:

- Alaska Plea Bargaining Study, 1974-1976
- Jury Verdicts Database for Cook County Illinois and All Counties in California, 1960-1984
- Legal Representation Data, 1970
- Survey of Tort Litigants in Three State Courts, 1989-1990: United States
- AIDS-Related Written Court Decisions in Federal and State Courts, 1984-1989: United States

All indicate the possible range of topics of study for those interested in legally related crime research.

## Mass Political Behavior and Attitudes

This category contains the second largest collection of databases available through the ICPSR. The majority of data sets focus on surveys taken during local, state, and federal elections. A fair number of databases also cover international elections and referendums. It is interesting to note that it is now possible to look at campaign expenditures for all candidates for federal office registered with the Federal Election Commission. In addition, data are available on all candidates and their committees, other political committees, and persons making independent expenditures. The data are made possible because of requests that have been processed under the federal Freedom of Information Act (see Chapter 6).

Aside from analyzing dimensions of elections, a large number of databases within this category are the results of polls taken by various media agencies (e.g., ABC news). The majority of these polls are relevant to crime researchers perhaps only to the extent that there are pertinent questions asked. Unfortunately, such questions in the polls in this category are rare and appear only tangential to the focus of the poll. Typical is the database "CBS News Polling America, March 17-19, 1991," which poses a variety of questions related to the economy, health, and foreign relations, but also includes a few questions to elicit opinions about the number of Americans who cheat on their income taxes.

## Social Indicators

Grouped within this category are the General Social Surveys. With three exceptions (1979, 1981, 1992), the General Social Survey has been conducted by the National Opinion Research Center annually since 1972. Each year the Roper Center for Public Opinion Research prepares a cumulative data set that merges previous years of the General Social Survey into a single file, with each year constituting a single sub-file. The primary topics surveyed include socioeconomic status, social mobility, social control, the family, race relations, sex relations, civil liberties, and morals. The survey population consists of those who speak English, are 18 years of age or older, and who live in non-institutional settings in the United States.

### Social Institutions and Behavior

Within this category is a series of annual surveys begun in 1976 and continuing today titled "Monitoring the Future: A Continuing Study of the Lifestyles and Values of Youth." The survey polls a nationally representative sample of high school seniors in the contiguous United States, asking approximately 100 drug use and demographic questions plus an average of 200 additional questions on a variety of subjects including attitudes toward government, social institutions, race relations, changing roles for women, educational aspirations, and occupational aims as well as marital and family plans. This survey frequently serves as a national guidepost on trends in juvenile drug use.

A similar set of surveys of parents and youth, available for the years 1976 through 1980 and 1983, more specifically examines the relationship of youth and delinquency, focusing on variables such as disruptive events in the home, neighborhood problems, parental aspirations for youth, labeling, attitudes toward deviance in adults and juveniles, parental discipline, and community involvement. The surveys are titled "National Youth Survey Series."

### Desktop Holdings

Many data sets are available on diskettes or CD-ROMs through ICPSR. In many instances, the data are available for immediate downloading as well as being available on compact disks or diskettes. In other instances, they are only available on compact disks or diskettes. Data sets available on the aforementioned medium include the following:

- Child Abuse, Neglect, and Violent Criminal Behavior in a Midwest Metropolitan Area of the United States, 1967-1988
- Criminal Careers of Juveniles in New York City, 1977-1983
- Factors Influencing the Quality and Utility of Government-Sponsored Criminal Justice Research in the United States, 1975-1986
- Armed Criminals in America: A Survey of Incarcerated Felons, 1983
- Improving Correctional Classification, New York, 1981-1983
- Exploring the House Burglar's Perspective: Observing and Interviewing Offenders in St. Louis, 1989-1990
- Community Policing in Madison, Wisconsin: Evaluation of Implementation and Impact, 1987-1990
- Nature and Patterns of Homicide in Eight American Cities, 1978
- Public and Private Resources in Public Safety [United States]: Metropolitan Area Panel Data, 1977 and 1982
- Robberies in Chicago, 1982-1983

## The National Archive of Criminal Justice Data (NACJD)

The National Archive of Criminal Justice Data (NACJD) *(http://www.icpsr.umich.edu/NACJD/welcome.html)* is a branch of the ICPSR at the University of Michigan. The mission of NACJD is to acquire, archive, process, and provide access to computer-readable criminal justice data collections for research and instruction. The NACJD web site provides downloadable access to more than 600 criminal justice data collections. NACJD has two major sponsors that archive data sets with them.

## Bureau of Justice Statistics

NACJD is primarily sponsored by the Bureau of Justice Statistics (BJS). BJS is a component of the Office of Justice Programs within the U.S. Department of Justice. While BJS collects (with the U.S. Census Bureau) National Criminal Victimization Survey data, it also collects, analyzes, publishes, and disseminates information on offenders, victims, and characteristics of the justice system at all levels of government. Some of the major data sets sponsored by BJS and archived at NACJD are

- Capital Punishment in the United States
- Census of State Adult Correctional Facilities
- Census of State and Local Law Enforcement Agencies
- Expenditure and Employment Data for the Criminal Justice System
- Monitoring of Federal Criminal Convictions and Sentences: Appeals Data, 1993-1996
- Monitoring of Federal Criminal Sentences
- National Corrections Reporting Program
- National Crime Victimization Survey
- National Jail Census
- National Judicial Reporting Program
- National Prosecutors Survey
- National Survey of Jails
- Organizations Convicted in Federal Criminal Courts
- State Court Processing Statistics
- Survey of Adults on Probation
- Survey of Inmates of Federal Correctional Facilities
- Survey of Inmates of Local Jails (formerly Survey of Jail Inmates)
- Survey of Inmates of State Correctional Facilities
- Uniform Crime Reporting Program Data

## National Institute of Justice

National Institute of Justice (NIJ)-sponsored research data are made available through the Data Resources Program. NIJ publishes a directory of data sources titled, appropriately enough, *Data Resources of the National Institute of Justice* (the 11th edition was the most recent at the time of this writing; NIJ, 1998). A copy is available at libraries that serve as government depositories or is available at *http:// www.icpsr.umich.edu/ICPSR/About/Publications/NACJD/nij98.pdf*. The current (1998) edition contains information on 266 NIJ data sets, contributed by 395 original principal investigators. Data from NIJ-sponsored research are deposited at NACJD and include data, codebooks, and other needed material. Some data sets available through NACJD are

- Effects of Legal Supervision of Chronic Addict Offenders in Southern California, 1974-1981
- Robbery of Financial Institutions in Indiana, 1982-1984
- Minimum Legal Drinking Age and Crime in the United States, 1980-1987
- Retail-Level Heroin Enforcement and Property Crime in 30 Cities in Massachusetts, 1980-1986
- Gang Involvement in "Rock" Cocaine Trafficking in Los Angeles, 1984-1985
- Criminal Careers and Crime Control in Massachusetts [The Glueck Study]: A Matched Longitudinal Research Design, Phase I, 1940-1965
- Changing Patterns of Drug Abuse and Criminality Among Crack Cocaine Users in New York City: Criminal Histories and Criminal Justice System Processing, 1983-1984, 1986
- Arrests Without Conviction, 1979-1980: Jacksonville and San Diego
- Individual Responses to Affirmative Action Issues in Criminal Justice Agencies, 1981: [United States]

- Residential Neighborhood Crime Control Project: Hartford, Connecticut, 1973, 1975-1977, 1979
- Phoenix [Arizona] Use of Force Project, June 1994
- Victim Impact Statements: Their Affects on Court Outcomes and Victim Satisfaction in New York, 1988-1990
- Drug Use Forecasting in 24 Cities in the United States, 1987-1992
- Nature and Sanctioning of White Collar Crime, 1976-1978
- Deterrent Effects of the New York Juvenile Offender Law, 1974-1984
- Effects of "United States v. Leon" on Police Search Warrant Practices, 1984-1985

## Summary

As indicated, housed within ICPSR and NACJD are a number of criminal justice archival projects. In addition to data from research sponsored by BJS and NIJ, data from the Office of Juvenile Justice and Delinquency Prevention, National Science Foundation, and other sponsoring agencies are archived at ICPSR. As page constraints make it impossible to describe all of the data sets available, the best method is either a careful exploration of ICPSR and NACJD archives or contacting one of the sponsoring agencies.

## Other Sources

Privately supported and non-profit agencies have a variety of policies governing the dissemination of secondary data. Some organizations routinely deposit their data with ICPSR; others make theirs available by contacting them. Some charge for a copy of their data; others offer selective access or make it free. In this section, a variety of different sources of secondary data are described that make available crime-related data.

## National Data Archive on Child Abuse and Neglect

The National Data Archive on Child Abuse and Neglect *(http://www.fldc.cornell.edu/)* is a project of the Family Life Development Center, College of Human Ecology, Cornell University.

The mission of the National Data Archive on Child Abuse and Neglect (NDACAN) is to facilitate the secondary analysis of research data relevant to the study of child abuse and neglect. By making data available to a larger number of researchers, NDACAN seeks to provide a relatively inexpensive and scientifically productive means for researchers to explore important issues in the child maltreatment field.

The maximum fee for each of the data sets is $75. Examples of the kind of data available are given below.

- Substantiation of Child Abuse and Neglect Reports, 1985
- National Family Violence Survey, 1985
- Fertility and Contraception Among Low-Income Child Abusing Mothers in Baltimore, MD, 1984-1985.
- Maltreatment and the Academic and Social Adjustment of School Children, 1987-1988

## United Nations Crime and Justice Information Network

The United Nations Crime and Justice Information Network web site *(http://www.ifs.univie~ac.at/~uncjin/wcs.html)* contains data sets for the First through Fifth United Nations Surveys of Crime Trends and Operations of Criminal Justice Systems (1970-1994). The data can be freely downloaded, but the user is cautioned to read the codebook carefully as there are always missing data and other problems in the use of international data. The United Nations Survey of Crime Trends and Operations of Criminal Justice Systems is available in ASCII, Lotus 123, and SPSS formats.

## Henry A. Murray Research Center of Radcliffe College

The Center's *(http://www.radcliffe.edu/murray/index.htm)* data holdings include studies with both female and male subjects from a wide range of ages and racial, ethnic, and socioeconomic class groups. These data were collected using a variety of methods, including longitudinal, cross-sectional, survey, case study, and experimental designs. The studies originate in all the social sciences; psychology, sociology, and education are especially well represented. In keeping with Radcliffe's mission to encourage research about women, topics of special concern to women are integral to the center's data collections. They include various aspects of women's work and careers, education, mental health, political participation, family life, widowhood, and aging. The center is particularly concerned with collecting data sets that include women of color, lesbians, and working-class women. It appears that data sets are available without charge, although there is an application process and a short research proposal requested. Crime-related data sets include

- Gluecks' Crime Causation Study: Unraveling Juvenile Delinquency
- The Harlem Longitudinal Study of Urban Black Youth
- Life Histories of Women in Prison

## The Federal Justice Statistics Program (FJSP)

The Federal Justice Statistics Program (FJSP) *(http://fjsrc.urban.org/index.shtml)* is part of the Urban Institute. The data sets are deposited with ICPSR (ICPSR 9096) and, except for the codebook, are open only to authorized users. With funding support from BJS, the FJSP compiles comprehensive information describing suspects and defendants processed in the Federal justice system.

FJSP provides uniform definitions and case processing statistics across all stages of the federal criminal justice system. Because the definitions used in FJSP are consistent with definitions used by other BJS programs, federal and state case processing statistics can be compared.

The FJSP database is constructed from data files provided by the following sources:

- Executive Office for U.S. Attorneys
- Administrative Office of the U.S. Courts
- U.S. Sentencing Commission
- Federal Bureau of Prisons

The Urban Institute receives data extracts regularly for each of the aforementioned agencies. The data extracts are disaggregated into one or more "standard analysis files" and are archived.

## National Center for Juvenile Justice

The National Center for Juvenile Justice *(http://www.ncjj.org/)* was founded in 1973 as the research division of the National Council of Juvenile and Family Court Judges. Its mission is to help children and families by conducting research and providing objective, factual information that is utilized to increase the juvenile and family justice systems' effectiveness. It specializes in data collection, research, and analyses; management information systems; technical assistance; and facility design guidelines and evaluation.

The National Center for Juvenile Justice's secondary data offering is unique. The "Easy Access" series is developed for research and non-technical professionals, distributed on 3.5" diskettes, and no additional statistical software is needed to examine the data. There are three diskettes available without charge:

- Easy Access to FBI Arrest Statistics 1994-1996
- Easy Access to Juvenile Court Statistics
- Easy Access to the FBI's Supplementary Homicide Reports: 1980-1996

## Statistical Analysis Centers

In contrast to the federal government, there is more variance in how individual states collect and disseminate data. A good place to start if one is interested in data collected by states is a state's Statistical Analysis Center (SAC), a federally designated agency that has responsibility for collecting criminal justice data. There is a good deal of variance in the amount and types of data collected, mostly dependent upon the size of the state, but SACs provide an initial starting point for those interested in state criminal justice data. For more information about SACs, users can view the web site *(http://www.jrsa.org/)* or contact them by mail (see the Appendix).

## A Final Word on Sources

While archival data on crime are abundant, the user should not overlook requesting secondary data sets from the originator. It is probably a redundant exercise for sponsored research projects, because the data will be deposited in an archive as a matter of course, but the official statistics and official records of many agencies have seen little more than limited administrative use and, therefore, represent a potential data source.

There are two issues that increase the chances of obtaining data from originating agencies. First, if the data are in machine-readable form, access is more likely because there are fewer problems of access and data collection than for paper files that require on-site transcription. Second, as was noted in Chapter 1, one of the differences between official records and official statistics is that the latter are designed for public consumption. Because a major mission of agencies that produce official statistics is to increase use of these data, they frequently welcome data requests from crime researchers.

For example, in a casual conversation with an employee of the California Criminal Justice Statistics Center, I mentioned that I had seen very little research on homicide in California. Her response was that they encouraged use of their records for research purposes, but they had received very few requests for their notably complete file on all reported homicides in the state. I requested, received, and formatted in SPSS a file of all California homicides from 1987 through 1997. As annual data become available, I add them to the master file. In agreement with the Center, I have documented the homicide data and made them available to other researchers. While it includes all the data requested in the Supplementary Homicide Reports, there are some additional variables collected by the California agency.

Perhaps the most surprising source of secondary data is persons who display an enormous amount of energy collecting detailed information on a topic using personal resources, for no other reason than an interest in the phenomenon. For example, there is the remarkably complete file of civil executions in the United States from 1608 through 1991 available from NACJD (ICPSR 8451). The file, known simply as the "Espy File," was started by a private citizen, M. Watt Espy of Headland, Alabama. Mr. Espy, using his own resources, started combing through every available historical account in 1970 for information on executions. In 1977, Mr. Espy's enterprise moved to the University of Alabama Law Center. Finally, in 1984, with the help of John Ortiz Smykla, a professor of criminal justice, and the cooperation of ICPSR, a grant was obtained from the National Science Foundation. Using these funds, the data were formatted, corrected, updated, and deposited at ICPSR.

Mr. Espy and Dr. Smykla have confirmed 14,634 executions performed in the United States under civil authority since 1608. The data set contains 21 variables that describe each individual executed and the circumstances surrounding the crime for which the person was convicted.

Because most crime research is done in the social sciences, where archived data are prominently available, it is easy to overlook one final source. Given the multidisciplinary character of crime research, future inquiries may want to explore medical, genetic, or other biological causes. Some journals in these disciplines require prospective authors to deposit data in an archive prior to acceptance of the articles. Hence, access to the data is through the auspices of journals rather than data archives.

## Building Data Sets On-Line

Among recent developments in the use of the Internet for crime research is the capacity to create a data set on-line tailored to a researcher's specific requirements. Using the National Archives of Criminal Justice Data *(http://www.icpsr.umich.edu/NACJD/)* to download a data file, codebook, and SPSS or SAS data definition files is time-consuming but within the capacities of most computer modem speeds and hard drive storage, provided the data set is not too large. While it may not be too time-consuming to download the 1996 Supplementary Homicide Reports *(http://www.icpsr.umich.edu/NACJD/ucr96.html#shr)*, which are approximately five megabytes, the time demands become excessive when a researcher wants to download 10 years of Supplementary Homicide Reports. In addition, some data sets are so large that downloading the entire data set is unrealistic. For example, the Uniform Crime Reports file on Offenses Known to the Police and Clearances by Arrest for one year, 1996, is approximately 69 megabytes *(http://www.icpsr.umich.edu/NACJD/ucr96.html#okca)*. The impracticality of downloading a massive data set is circumvented by constructing a data set on-line that meets particular research requirements and downloading it. Three on-line data construction systems are discussed next.

## Data Analysis System

The first is the Data Analysis System of the National Archive of Criminal Justice Data *(http://www.icpsr.umich.edu/NACJD/SDA/ das.html)*. The Data Analysis System enables the user to create subsets of data that can be analyzed by SPSS or SAS. At this time, available data sets include the 1996 Supplementary Homicide Reports, 1995 and 1996 UCR County-level Detailed Arrest and Offense Data, a detailed data set of homicides in Chicago from 1965 through 1995, 1996 National Crime Victimization Survey, 1991 Survey of Inmates of State Correctional Institutions, and several data sets from the National Corrections Reporting Program. Substance abuse and mental health data sets are also available for on-line selection and analysis. Other data sets are under construction.

Statistical analysis of a specified data set is possible using the Data Analysis System. Simple analyses include running frequencies, cross-tabulation, comparing means, and computing correlations. Options available in all analysis programs include modifying or restricting variables and using a control variable, a filter variable to select cases for analysis, and a weight variable.

After a customized data set is constructed, it is useful to download it in a format that can be used by the analysis software. In addition to SPSS, SAS, and SDA files, the Data Analysis System allows downloading as an ASCII file with none, blank, or comma delimiters.

## CDC Wonder

The second location where data sets can be constructed on-line is CDC Wonder *(http://wonder.cdc.gov/Welcome.html)*. CDC Wonder is sponsored by the Centers for Disease Control and Prevention, and many of the large number of files are health related such as information on AIDS, tuberculosis, and cancer. For the crime researcher, the site makes available census material for 1970, 1980, and 1990 with estimates for inter-censal years. Likewise, homicide data are available from the mortality files. Data sets can be constructed for years, nations, states, counties, gender, age, and racial groups. CDC Wonder-constructed data sets can be downloaded as ASCII, HTML, or comma delimited text files.

## U.S. Census Bureau

The U.S. Census Bureau makes its data available through archives, but it provides a number of data access tools and data at its own web site *(http://www.census.gov/main/www/access.html)*. FERRET (Federal Electronic Research and Review Extraction Tool) is a tool developed and supported by the U.S. Bureau of the Census in collaboration with the Bureau of Labor Statistics and other statistical agencies. After the user signs in with an e-mail address, FERRET takes the user through a series of steps from selecting the population data set to selecting variables. The user can view all or part of the data on the screen before downloading them as an ASCII file.

The Data Extraction System is another on-line tool for creating subsets of data from census files, including Current Population Surveys. Unlike FERRET, it does not do any type of simple statistical analysis, but is used to access data sets that can be downloaded and analyzed by statistical software.

The 1990 Census LOOKUP is an experimental inter-active tool for retrieving data from 1990 U.S. Census Summary Tape Files. Among the choices is creating a data set by zip code. After the zip code is entered, variables are chosen, and the data can be downloaded as an HTML, comma delimited ASCII, or CODATA file.

The ease of access and use of the three sites for constructing data sets on-line is similar. The major difference is that the Data Analysis system of NACJD has to be available for a larger variety of data sets. Both CDC Wonder and the census site focus primarily on official data that, in many instances, are highly standardized. The Data Analysis System has to be capable of assembling data sets from surveys, official records, and official statistics.

# APPENDIX
## ADDRESSES OF SECONDARY DATA SOURCES

**National Archives of Criminal Justice Data** (NACJD)
The University of Michigan
Institute for Social Research
426 Thompson St.
Ann Arbor, MI 48104-2321

*Mailing Address*
P.O. Box 1248
Ann Arbor, MI 48106-1248

**Bureau of Justice Statistics** (BJS)
810 Seventh Street, NW
Washington, DC 20531

**National Institute of Justice** (NIJ)
810 Seventh Street, NW
Washington, DC 20531

**National Data Archive on Child Abuse and Neglect**
Attention: Data Orders
Family Life Development Center
MVR Hall
Cornell University
Ithaca, NY 14853-4401

**United Nations Crime and Justice Information Network** (UNCJIN)
Centre for International Crime Prevention
Office for Drug Control and Crime Prevention
P.O. Box 500, A-1400
Vienna, Austria

**The Urban Institute**
2100 M Street, NW
Washington, DC 20037

**National Center for Juvenile Justice**
710 Fifth Avenue
Pittsburgh, PA 15219

**Henry A. Murray Research Center**
A Center for the Study of Lives
Radcliffe College
10 Garden St.
Cambridge, MA 02138

**Justice Research and Statistics Association**
444 North Capitol Street, NW, Suite 445
Washington, D.C. 20001

# DOING RESEARCH WITH SECONDARY DATA

Doing research with secondary data is similar to doing research with primary data. However, when using secondary data, during construction of the hypotheses it is important to consider what constraints a data set may impose on how questions can be answered. This chapter addresses hypothesis formulation and offers guidelines for evaluating official records and official statistics.

## Getting Started

Regardless of the type of data used, research begins with an idea. Unfortunately, there is no agreed-upon best method for generating ideas. According to Max Weber (1946b), "Ideas occur to us when they please, not when it pleases us" (p. 136). Louis Pasteur suggested that, "In the fields of observation, chance favors only the prepared mind" (cited in Hyman, 1972, p. 90).

Unfortunately, neither Weber nor Pasteur was more specific than suggesting that thinking and reading widely about a subject matter will help researchers hit upon an initial idea. Because ideas are stimulated in many different ways, crime researchers need to expose themselves to as many sources as possible. Popular sources include newspapers, magazines, journals, television, radio, the Internet, and discussions with friends and colleagues. A fair number of research ideas come from reading articles outside one's own discipline.

The potential of the Internet as a source for scholarly work is just being realized. Putting in key words in any one of a number of search engines will generate thousands of locations that can be explored. For example, using Yahoo, a popular search engine, the key word "capital punishment" elicited 111,745 locations to check for further information. The UnCover Company *(http://uncweb.carl.org/)* is another good source of information. This bibliographic service covers more than 17,000 multidisciplinary journals published since 1988. Searching can be done on the Internet or through libraries.

Practitioners in criminal justice agencies are another valuable source for research ideas. They may have excellent ideas, but are unable to pursue them because of job responsibilities. They may later be helpful in efforts to gain access to data. In addition, consider written accounts of people who work in criminal justice doing the kind of work related to a possible research topic. For example, an indication of how homicides are reported and investigated, and offenders arrested, is given by David Simon (1991), a reporter who followed a Baltimore homicide unit for a year. Simon's book, *Homicide: A Year on the Killing Streets,* was the basis of the television series *Homicide.* More recently, Miles Corwin (1997), a reporter for the *Los Angeles Times,* gave a thoughtful account of the work of homicide detectives in that city.

Regardless of how researchers arrive at their research topic, it is important to consider the full range of opinions and facts that surround it. Often, what sounds like a useful and interesting idea is found lacking in more thoughtful, scholarly articles. When it appears that an idea has merit, it is time to look carefully at the research literature.

## Forming Hypotheses:
## Reviewing Research Literature

What Borg and Gall (1979) have to say about literature reviews in educational research is equally applicable to research on crime:

> The review of the literature in educational research provides you with the means of getting to the frontier in your particular field of knowledge. Until you have learned what others have done and what remains still to be done in your area, you cannot develop a research project that will contribute to furthering knowledge in your field. Thus the literature in any field forms the foundation upon which all future work must be built. If you fail to build this foundation of knowledge, provided by the review of the literature, your work is likely to be shallow and naive, and will often duplicate work that has already been done better by someone else. Although the importance of a thorough review of the literature is obvious to everyone, this task is more frequently slighted than any other phase of research. (p. 98)

It is important in the early stages of exploring research literature not to define the topic too narrowly too soon. Too narrow a definition of the topic leads researchers to believe that they are opening a new line of inquiry when, in fact, it is merely conceptualized differently elsewhere. For example, if a researcher wants to review the literature on police clearances, that is, the process by which investigations and arrests occur, studying police behavior and patterns of investigation is logical. Considering the extensive literature on crime prevention programs designed to increase the number of arrests is also important, because they have a bearing on arrest clearances.

As researchers continue to explore the research literature, their interests take on a sharper focus. Some parts of a general idea may have little merit, other parts may be uninteresting, and still others may lead into areas that are not feasible to pursue. Gradually, an initial idea assumes shape, and possible hypotheses emerge. The process of narrowing a general idea to a specific researchable question is often a very stimulating experience. Many researchers lament the fact there are so many interesting, worthwhile questions to pursue, but so little time and so few resources available to pursue them. If only we could answer all the questions we ask!

It is important when considering possible hypotheses to recognize that they are two-faced, like the Roman god Janus. One face looks toward the significance of the research while the other looks toward methodology and data sources. The significance of the research refers to its meaning and importance in a broader social and theoretical context. Simply put, what difference do the results of the research make? Is it relevant to testing some key propositions of a theory? Does it contribute to a better understanding or use of an existing social practice or policy? Does it bring into question a widely held belief about criminal behavior? Is there a flaw in the way previous research was done that distorts the findings and can be remedied in the proposed research? The research literature is used to provide a basis of support and belief to justify this line of inquiry rather than another.

To understand what is meant by putting hypotheses in the context of a theoretical or policy issue, consider the problem of justifiable homicides. Why should anyone be interested in studying justifiable homicides? They are a small number of killings, 5% or less, for which prosecutors have ruled there is no criminal liability (Alvarez, 1992). However, an examination of the research literature shows the relevance of justifiable homicides to three important issues: (a) the use of deadly force by police (Fyfe, 1982; Geller, 1982); (b) the use of lethal force by civilians (Kleck, 1988; Tennenbaum, 1993); and (c) justifiable homicide pleas by battered women (Gillespie, 1989). Thus, what might appear at first glance as an insignificant number has important policy implications.

A review of the literature does not guarantee significant hypotheses or substantive research. Ordinary people, who may be unfamiliar with a body of research literature, sometimes have important and creative ideas that lead to substantive contributions. Creativity in understanding crime is certainly not limited to those who read journals. Nor is advocating a review of relevant research literature intended to discourage new and innovative approaches to research. Researchers should not slavishly use approaches and methods that are found in published literature simply because they are "acceptable." Innovation and improvements need to be preceded by an understanding of what was done and why. An open mind is not, after all, the same as an empty head!

The other face of hypotheses looks toward how they can be tested. Hypotheses are statements of anticipated relationships between two or more variables. By definition, hypotheses must be testable, which means that there must be some way, through systematic observation, that the relationships can be shown to be supported or not supported. The variety of methods for doing the latter are covered in most introductory courses on research methods.

What distinguishes secondary data users at this stage is that crime researchers have to allow for the nature of a known data set in formulating hypotheses and a research plan for testing them. The hard fact is that research designs using secondary data are limited by what is available in the files. As Hakim (1983) has noted about official records, a different approach must be used:

> The main feature of records-based studies is that the records exist already and cannot be created to the researcher's specification. The approach to research design has to be back-to-front. Instead of designing the study, and then collecting data in accordance with it, one gets full details of how the data was collected and/or recorded, and then *identifies (or recognizes) the research model* to which it corresponds. (italics in the original; p. 504)

To an extent, the kinds of research models associated with a given data set are shown in the available research literature. Research on homicide, for example, relies on correlational designs showing patterns of offending and victimization. In addition to hypotheses, the research literature shows a variety of measurements, research designs, and analysis approaches that might be used. How the data were collected and/or recorded affords the secondary data user the opportunity to evaluate relevance and quality of the data. This topic is addressed in the following sections.

There are three questions that need to be answered as a result of evaluating the literature and refining ideas into hypotheses. First, is the proposed research the next logical step in view of what has already been done? Of course, there are many "next logical steps," but the question is whether the relevant research literature can support the conclusion that this is one of them.

Second, consider the outcome of testing hypotheses from a "worst case" perspective. Is the outcome just as important if the results are completely contrary to what is hypothesized? If so, what does that mean? Do the contrary results support an entirely different explanation? Do they open a new line of inquiry? Do contrary results show that previous research is limited to using certain types of research methods? If there are substantive answers to the preceding questions, the research hypotheses will lead to an important contribution. If not, then critics are inclined to ask why the research effort was made in the first place, particularly when the results run counter to the researchers' expectations.

Third, can the secondary data source support the research inquiry? Are the data available to test the hypotheses? For example, data examining daily variations in homicide are not available from official statistics like the Supplementary Homicide Reports, but they may be collected by state criminal justice statistics agencies. What about the myriad reliability and validity questions about the data? In what follows, issues are considered relating to evaluating official records and the UCR Program as an instance of official statistics.

## Evaluating Secondary Data Sources

In this discussion of the two types of secondary data, the reader needs to be aware that answers to the questions posed will be obtained in different ways and times. For official records, some answers can be obtained by talking to people who have used the same agency sources. Other answers are best provided by people who manage record systems in agencies. Such discussions may take place as part of the process of accessing official records as discussed in Chapter 4. Information on official statistics, on the other hand, is available from handbooks, annual reports, and other types of documentation freely available from agencies that compile and disseminate the data.

## Official Records

### Legal and Social Background

The first step in learning the strengths and limitations of official records is to examine the legal and social backgrounds of agencies collecting the data. Learning about the goals of an agency provides clues as to the kind of data found because the authority to collect information is part of the major activities and mission of that agency. Police, for example, collect information that will support reporting crime, investigation, and apprehension. Likewise, prisons, detention centers, probation offices, and courts collect data that support their social service functions.

The goals of agencies are important in defining the unit of observation in official records, that is, their definition of a "case." Law enforcement data typically use victim complaints as the building blocks of official records, but not all victim-based systems are the same.

Within a victim-based system, there may be important variations in what is collected. Police collect data on homicide because it is a crime, but for medical examiners it is a mortality phenomenon where the major interest is the cause of death. What Rand (1993) has noted for official statistics is also applicable to police and medical examiner records:

> differences between cases in the files are to a great degree the result of differences in the two programs' purposes and procedures. Basically, the UCR measures crimes, of which death is one outcome. The Mortality System measures deaths, of which crime is one cause. (p. 112)

The focus of the official records of medical examiners and coroners is medically supported decisions about the cause of death of victims. There is very little information about offenders, circumstances surrounding the acts, and the legal character of killings. Police department data, on the other hand, contain information on both victims and offenders, circumstances, justifiable homicide by civilians and police, murder and non-negligent manslaughters, and negligent manslaughters (Riedel, 1999).

The types and quality of data are also influenced by how central the event is to the agency's goals and activities. For example, police departments are more concerned with violent felonies than misdemeanors. Therefore, homicides are going to receive more attention and have better records than gambling offenses.

The amount and quality of official records are affected by the amount of the crime. For example, there will be few records on marijuana possession for single individuals unless the arrests occur in conjunction with more serious felonies. On the other hand, a network of buying and selling marijuana that leads to several arrests will interest urban law enforcement.

Agencies have an input and output side in interacting with their organizational environment. On the input side, how do cases come under their jurisdiction? Do agency personnel depend on public cooperation for information or do they receive information from other agencies? Detention centers, courts, prisons, and treatment centers are examples of agencies that receive their input from law enforcement and other agencies. The preceding questions are important because they define the segment of the population that will be available for analysis. Prisons, for example, contain a higher proportion of stranger murder offenders than police data because stranger murder offenders are more likely to be incarcerated (Gottfredson & Gottfredson, 1988).

On the output side, where do cases and associated data go after they leave the agency? To whom are agencies accountable? As a rule, information that goes to other agencies pursuant to their missions is collected more carefully. For example, police collect data from the viewpoint of "making a case," that is, a case that will be prosecuted. Denoting the type and quality of evidence, interviews with witnesses, and compliance with legal requirements for arrest are relevant to subsequent prosecution and are collected carefully.

There are two reasons for considering the legal and social backgrounds of agencies. First, knowing about agency goals and activities helps in understanding the limitations of the data. This not only includes the range and type of information collected, but it may also provide hypotheses about over-reporting and under-reporting vis-à-vis similar agencies. Moreover, understanding the backgrounds of agencies helps provide a richer context for evaluating the significance and generalizability of research questions.

Second, what is learned about the legal and social background of the data source may be relevant to gaining access to certain types of official records. There are legal and administrative limits to the kinds of data made available for research purposes. Some states prohibit release of criminal history information, and information about juveniles is typically not available without a court order. It's unlikely that agencies will allow access to cases currently being processed. Likewise, agencies may not release information about cases that make sources of information vulnerable, such as organized crime informants.

### What Is Collected?

At the outset, it is important to get an overview of how agencies process cases. A flowchart of decisions and alternatives available for which there are records is important. A useful tactic is to obtain blank copies of all the forms used by an agency and use them as a basis for asking questions about the progress of a case through the agency. The answers to the questions provide a basis for charting the flow.

Generally, at each decision point, cases are carried on to either the next point of agency processing or they are diverted from the system. Diversions from the system can occur for a variety of reasons. When citizens enter complaints to the police that crimes have occurred, police investigate and decide whether complaints are "founded." "Unfounded complaints" mean that no crimes have occurred or there is no foundation for further investigation, and events leave the system. Diversions can also mean that after preliminary investigation, cases may be referred to social service agencies better suited to the complaints.

Diverted cases are important to examine because they help to establish the limits of generalizations. Where possible, crime researchers should attempt to get information on the number and circumstances of the cases diverted from the system. For minor crimes and juveniles, police frequently use their discretion to avoid entering cases into the formal system. Similarly, in looking at violations in correctional settings, some infractions may systematically be overlooked. Such cases are typically lost to the record system, although it is worth exploring by interview what percentage of cases is lost in that fashion. Obviously, for serious and violent offenses, little diversion occurs.

### How Are Records Organized?

Are cases filed alphabetically, by the date they come under the jurisdiction of the agency, by the type of event, or by initial action taken? How they are organized will have a decided impact on the ease with which a sample can be drawn and data collection organized. Perhaps the most important feature to discover is when the information is recorded. If agencies are complacent in recording information for files, there may be a greater chance for inaccuracies. The greater the time lapse, the greater the potential for mistakes.

### What Holds the Case Together?

Cases can be held together in two different ways. Are there unique case identifiers (numerical and otherwise) that link different forms used to record a target's progress through the agency? These unique identifiers may be a numerical system used by agencies, a docket, or indictment numbers. Where there are no unique identifiers, researchers may be faced with the onerous task of matching records by using the name, age, race, and/or gender of a person.

There are also event identifiers. Given an incident involving several victims and/or offenders occurring in a circumscribed time and location, is it possible to identify these cases? Both case and event identifiers should be noted by the data user for later reference.

### What Is the Item Level of Specification?

In the opinion of knowledgeable sources, what percentage of the forms have complete information on each item? What percentage of the specific item is complete? For example, an item may request both weapon used and, if a firearm, caliber. While a high percentage of responses is indicated for weapons, calibers are noted less frequently. Where the completion rate is low, researchers may conclude the item is not worth incorporating in the data collection form.

### How Are Missing Data Shown?

Do the records distinguish between questions asked in which the respondent does not know, questions never asked, and questions asked but answers recorded elsewhere? The distinction is important because information not found in one form may be found in another. For example, forms are repetitive in their demands for information like age, race, and gender. Blank spaces on one form may not mean an absence of information, but simply that it can be found on another form in the dossier. On the other hand, the responses to the item may be so unreliable that interviewers have simply stopped asking.

### What Kind of Documentation Is Available?

Are there agency-wide keys, classifications, or codebooks that identify standard notations, abbreviations, or codes used in the records? The records of many criminal justice agencies contain abbreviated information that speed completion of records. These include describing legal charges with initials, such as "A & B" for "Assault and Battery," or using notations that indicate their locations in the criminal code. Where such abbreviations are a consistent practice, copies of whatever translation device is used will be needed to construct a data collection instrument.

### What Collateral Information Is Available?

Collateral information refers to information that has a bearing on cases at hand, but comes from other sources. For example, information on prior arrests, convictions, and dispositions is sometimes included in police files, but is taken from data sources outside the agency.

There are two types of collateral information that need to be evaluated. As a rule, information about the subject's behavior *before* his or her appearance in the target agency is more reliably recorded than information *after* the person has left the agency. Prior information (previous arrests, convictions, and dispositions) is more consistently recorded because it is used for subsequent legal processing. On the other hand, collateral information on the outcome of cases may not be a concern of the agency, which means that information will be collected sporadically and inconsistently.

## How Are Data Stored and Accessed?

Agencies use paper files, electronic storage and access, or a combination of the two. In the latter instance, agencies may make frequently used information available by computer and more detailed records in less accessible paper files.

Where the needed data are available as computer records, it is necessary to consider how the data can be transferred from agency systems to systems capable of doing statistical analyses. Sometimes, agencies have the capability for statistical analyses; usually, however, researchers have to explore data formats recognized by two different systems or convert from one data format to another.

The usual problem is determining whether agency records can be used with computer-based statistical analysis packages such as SPSS-PC or SAS. Agency formats can be altered or converted with computer programs, such as macros for text editors like Kedit. It is advisable to spend time exploring the technical complexities of converting from one format to another. Using electronic storage and access will reduce the time needed to create a data file and will minimize errors that result from any manual approach.

## Who Does the Collecting?

*Recorders* is a generic term for persons who complete the forms, organize the information, maintain the record system, and make the information available as needed. For official records, there are two types of recorders. In an ongoing agency, service delivery persons such as police officers, social workers, probation officers, and correctional officers also have the responsibility of completing forms detailing their decisions and activities. The second type of recorders are those for whom record keeping is a full-time occupation. They include positions like file clerks and managers, data processing personnel, and computer operators and programmers.

Who initially completes the forms? If they are service delivery persons, is completing records evaluated as an important part of their job? Is time routinely set apart from their other tasks to complete records? What kind of training and supervision are they given?

The above questions are particularly important where the completion of forms requires a written narrative. For example, police officers generally provide a highly standardized narrative of the criminal incident. Beyond those characteristics readily observed, how do police officers make decisions about more elusive matters? For example, a puzzling feature of homicide research is how police officers decide, before an arrest is made, that the homicide was committed by a stranger (Riedel, 1993).

What is the nature of the training and supervision for full-time recorders? Do they review the forms completed by service delivery persons for accuracy and consistency? Do full-time recorders and service delivery persons cooperate in maintaining files?

Where the record-keeping system is highly computerized, it is important to know how the information is entered into the computer. Is this done by service delivery persons or at a later stage by full-time recorders? What are the procedures to check on accuracy and consistency of entry?

Information about the behavior of recorders serves to inform expectations about quality of the data. Where there is little training and supervision, poor relationships between recorders and service delivery persons, a low priority assigned to record keeping, or the tasks given little status in the agency, records may not support the proposed research inquiry. On the other hand, where the opposite is true, not only will records be of higher quality, but researchers will be more likely to receive help from recorders during the data collection phase.

### Changes, Beginnings, and Endings

Have there been any changes in the record-keeping system? These changes may be either periodic or unforeseen. Periodic shifts include elimination or introduction of a form or revisions in existing forms because of routine review. Unforeseen changes in the record system are generally responses to major shifts in the agency mandate or in management of the record-keeping system. This can include the hiring of new personnel or movement of the record-keeping function from one agency to another.

Changes in a record system pose a major problem for compatibility between research data gathered before and after the change. The simplest changes are where the item remains, but one version asks for less information than the other. For example, if the original version classifies race as "white" and "nonwhite," while the revised item classifies a number of different races, the problem can be resolved by using the dichotomy.

Where one item is revised to incorporate the information contained in several earlier items, the problem is more complex. One solution is to compare results on the revised and unrevised versions and empirically determine the amount of compatibility between the two items. Where there are changes in the record-keeping system resulting in major incompatibilities, researchers may have to limit themselves to the most recent version of the record system.

Being aware of the beginning date and implementation time for variables with a short collection history is also important. For example, examining the effect of changes in firearms laws may not be possible until a law has been implemented for some time. In addition to the time required for cases to accumulate, there is the inevitable confusion associated with changes in record keeping.

Similarly, it is important to learn the approximate time needed for a case to be processed by agencies and establish a cutoff point that will include only completed cases. Because it is unlikely that researchers will have access to cases currently under investigation, including recent cases in the sample is likely to introduce a bias by excluding those not available.

The importance of these questions and guidelines for evaluating official records cannot be overlooked. Responding to these concerns provides a basis for defining the quality of the data and the generalizability of any subsequent analyses.

## Official Statistics and the UCR Program

### Legal and Social Characteristics

Agencies collecting official statistics operate under legislative mandates provided by either federal or state legislation, depending upon the agencies. For example, the UCR Program and the National Center for Health Statistics (NCHS) operate under laws provided by the U.S. Congress. State agencies receive legislative authority from their respective lawmaking bodies. In Illinois, the state police have legislative authority to collect crime data from local jurisdictions. In California, the state agency is the Criminal Justice Statistics Center, which is part of the California Department of Justice.

Official statistics agencies gather data through cooperative arrangements with local and state agencies. Early in its history, the NCHS developed birth and death certificates as reporting devices and promoted a system of state offices of vital statistics that would, in turn, gather data from local agencies. Consequently, NCHS assumes complete coverage since 1933, uses no estimates, and all published data are considered final and not subject to revision (Cantor & Cohen, 1980).

The UCR Program began in the 1930s as a voluntary reporting system between law enforcement agencies and the FBI, which became the clearinghouse for crime data. In the past few decades, the UCR Program has also promoted a program of statewide agencies gathering crime information and reporting to the federal program. By 1993, 44 states and the District of Columbia had statewide reporting systems. The remaining jurisdictions report directly to the UCR Program (Riedel, 1999).

The unit of observation for NCHS is victims, and relevant information is collected on a single document, a standardized death certificate. For the UCR, there are three major forms: Offenses Known to the Police (Return A); Age, Sex, Race, and Ethnic Origin of Arrested Offenders; and the Supplementary Homicide Reports. Return A includes such items as whether the offense is "founded"; type of crime; and whether the offense was "cleared," that is, someone arrested. Age, Sex, Race, and Ethnic Origin of Arrested Offenders includes what the name indicates. Both of the preceding are total monthly numbers for each category when they are forwarded to the UCR Program.

The Supplementary Homicide Report (SHR) is a case-by-case report of homicides including age, gender, race, and ethnic origin of victims and offenders. Also included on the SHR are weapons used, circumstances of offenses, number of victims and offenders, and victim-offender relationships. Forms are also forwarded monthly to the UCR.

The UCR Program is an example of an official statistics data source and is the focus of subsequent discussion. It assumed its present shape in response to social and economic limitations. In the face of many local law enforcement agencies operating under a variety of state statutes, a program emphasizing cooperative relationships with state and local agencies is a reasonable solution. In short, managing reporting relationships with a small number of state programs is easier for a federal agency than managing a large number of local law enforcement units. Further, state agencies are in a better political and legal position than a federal agency to compel crime reporting from local units. There are, however, a number of disadvantages, noted below, that have an impact on the usefulness of the data.

### Definitional Issues and Reporting Relationships

In establishing a national reporting system, the UCR program defined crimes in ways that combined a variety of state statutes. Because of the variety of statutory inclusions and exclusions, it is difficult to know whether, for example, robbery in one state is comparable behavior to robbery in another state. One solution is to examine state reports to decide whether they describe what state laws are included in UCR definitions. Such considerations are essential where jurisdictional comparisons are anticipated.

It's also useful in evaluating UCR data to learn about the local, state, and national reporting relationships. Some states and agencies have reliably reported to the UCR Program for years with weak or no legislation. Others report because of statewide legislation, although the legislation varies as to sanctions available for non-compliance. For example, in 1991, 30 states had legislation mandating reporting by law enforcement agencies, but only 15 of the statutes specify penalties for non-compliance (Biderman & Lynch, 1991).

Some states indicate how much reporting: Illinois gives the total number of agencies reporting and lists the names of agencies that do not report to the state agency (Illinois State Police, 1995). Crime researchers have to assess the importance of the omissions. Because there are a small number of small jurisdictions not reporting in Illinois, their omission is unlikely to be a serious problem when considering serious violent crime. Research on other types of crimes may pose problems.

### What Is Reported?

The system of collection has an impact on what and how crime data are reported to national agencies. Providing state agencies and the UCR Program with local data is done at the expense of local resources. Understandably, local agencies want to minimize that expenditure where they perceive no direct agency benefit. As mentioned in Chapter 1, official statistics will contain much less detailed information than official records.

National agencies attempt to respond effectively and efficiently. Given the large amount of variation in what is collected locally, the UCR Program focuses on collecting information on a small number of variables that are general and can be validly and reliably collected.

Thus, while national data on gang activity would be useful, definitions of gangs and gang activity vary among jurisdictions.

In addition, this means that information may be available only in an aggregated form that precludes certain types of analysis. As noted previously, crimes known to the police are aggregated on a monthly basis when reported to the UCR Program. Similarly, arrests are aggregated monthly by the age, race, and gender of offenders. Homicides are the only offenses reported in detailed case-level fashion.

### Lost Cases and Lost Variables

Not all crimes are reported to the police. What is of concern is whether crimes reported to the police are reported to state agencies and the UCR Program. For example, the number of cases recorded from the Supplementary Homicide Reports is always less than that recorded on Return A (Riedel, 1999). In addition, unwritten policies may dictate that minor violations go unrecorded, conflicts and crimes between relatives and family members may be "informally" adjusted and no report filed, victims may file complaints but wish to take no official actions, and complainants may be hostile toward police. These and additional problems are discussed in greater detail elsewhere (Biderman & Lynch, 1991; Schneider & Wiersema, 1990).

Police departments do not always file reports for the full 12 months. When that occurs, the UCR Program uses an imputation process to estimate the missing information for the missing months. The imputation process has not been examined thoroughly; the only study known to the author is Schneider and Wiersema (1990).

In addition to lost cases, not all information is recorded. The UCR Program follows the "Hierarchy Rule" where, if several crimes are committed simultaneously, only the offense judged most serious is recorded; other offenses are ignored. The only exception is arson, which is counted when committed with another offense. For other recording practices, see Biderman and Lynch (1991) and O'Brien (1985).

Information requested may not be received. For example, Riedel (1993) found there were fewer stranger homicides reported on the SHR than reported by eight urban police departments. Because stranger homicides take longer to clear by arrest, there may be a reporting lag where victim-offender relationships are recorded as unknown on the monthly SHR. When the case is solved, victim-offender relationships are recorded in police records, but not forwarded to the UCR Program.

### Quality Control

Because official statistics agencies depend upon state and local sources, they have little direct control over the quality of the data they receive. Locally, there is enormous variation in the amount of care taken at the initial data entry point. The variation ranges from no review at all in some departments to sophisticated dual reporting systems. At the state and federal level, edit checks are carried out.

For the UCR, these data control techniques are

> particularly good at identifying errors in computation as well as keypunching and some coding errors. They are less well suited for detecting falsification, omission of descriptive information in the original report, and misclassification of incidents due to incomplete or erroneous information on the original offense report. Only full-scale audits could provide such information routinely. (Biderman & Lynch, 1991, p. 7)

### Documentation

Biderman and Lynch (1991) observe that much less discretion is left to the person completing NCVS forms in comparison to data gathered by UCR. In terms of structuring discretion with detailed instructions, the authors note, "The *Uniform Crime Reporting Handbook*, which explains the procedures for classifying, scoring, and submitting data to the UCR, is 89 pages. The *NCS Interviewer Manual* contains 552 pages" (p. 70).

The authors acknowledge a major difference between the two data systems: NCVS interviewers are employed, trained, and supervised by the U.S. Census. Data received by the UCR Programs comes from a multitude of local and state agency personnel who are not economically, and sometimes not legally, beholden to the FBI.

Documentation is a major weakness of a reporting system that depends on local and state agencies. Sherman and Langworthy (1979) note that there is a lack of awareness, concern, and support among coroners and medical examiners for complying with legal requests to complete death certificates using codes for the causes of death requested by NCHS. They also note that instructions for completing death certificates are vague and incomplete.

For the UCR, interviews with representatives of 42 state programs and 19 local or county police departments indicated problems that could be resolved with better documentation. These problems include incorrectly applying classification and offense counting rules, incomplete records, and downgrading offenses to make them less serious offenses in the UCR index (Abt Associates, 1984).

From the viewpoint of research users, there is almost no information about the reporting history of jurisdictions. There is no documentation on which jurisdictions submit full-year reports, less than full-year reports, and no reports. Where estimates are made for missing data, knowing the reported values to assess the impact of estimations would be useful.

There is a tendency for reported figures to fluctuate by small amounts, depending on the different sources. One reason is that the UCR Program will accept reports, at least those for homicide, up to one year after the annual report is published. After that, unless there is a major change, such as a large city turning in a missing month, the master files remain unchanged. Unfortunately, these changes are not documented (Riedel, 1999).

## National Incident-Based Reporting System (NIBRS)

The National Incident-Based Reporting System (NIBRS) originated as the outcome of an effort in 1982 by an FBI/Bureau of Justice Statistics task force to do a comprehensive evaluation and redesign of the UCR Program. The first two phases of a grant awarded to Abt Associates were focused on what changes were needed, while the third phase focused on implementing the recommended changes (Akiyama & Rosenthal, 1990; Poggio, Kennedy, Chaiken, & Carlson, 1985).

Except for the SHR, the traditional UCR system relies on counts of incidents and arrests. NIBRS is designed to gather detailed information on 46 Group A offenses in 22 categories such as robbery, types of homicides, assaults, sex offenses, fraud, and stolen property offenses. Group A offenses were selected, in part, because of their seriousness, frequency, prevalence, and visibility to law enforcement. Group B offenses consist of 11 less serious offense categories including bad check offenses, curfew violations, disorderly conduct, and drunkenness. For Group A crimes, a detailed incident report is filed, while only an arrest report is filed for Group B crimes (Federal Bureau of Investigation [FBI], 1992).

When fully implemented, NIBRS will provide much more data and in greater detail than is currently available from the SHR and summary data sources. Among the most important additions for Group A crimes are that

1.  each incident contains information on 52 variables covering characteristics of offenses, victims, offenders, and arrestees (Jarvis, 1992);
2.  all segments of the incident will be linked together with originating agency identifiers, incident numbers, and sequence numbers where multiple victims and offenders are involved;
3.  the hierarchy rule is no longer used; information on up to 10 offenses, 999 victims, and 99 offenders will be gathered;

4. information will be available on offenses cleared and exceptionally cleared, offenses attempted and completed, drug and/or alcohol use, bias crime involvement, type of premise entry, and property crime characteristics;

5. victim data will include resident status, type of victims and injuries, and specific relationship to each offender in multiple victim/offender cases;

6. codes for age, race, ethnicity, and gender of arrestees, dates of arrest, codes to distinguish arrests for each offense, whether arrestees were armed and weapon, types of resident status, and disposition of arrestees under 18;

7. whether incident reports are initial or supplemental, which permits updating of the files (FBI, 1992); and

8. three volumes of detailed documentation and a NIBRS version of the *UCR Handbook* to help data contributors (Federal Bureau of Investigation, 1996).

NIBRS data are not generally available in NIBRS format because of the process of development and implementation; data from participating states are currently included in existing UCR publications. Ten states are now supplying crime data in NIBRS format. An additional 22 states, three local law enforcement agencies in other states, and three federal agencies have submitted test tapes with data in NIBRS format. No date is given for final implementation.

## A Final Word

This chapter has focused on several elements of doing research with secondary data. Research begins with an idea derived from a variety of sources: print and television media, the Internet, and discussions with colleagues and practitioners. An idea begins to assume shape as a hypothesis as a result of reviewing the research literature, learning what elements of the original idea are worth pursuing, and how others have conceptualized them.

Hypotheses are Janus-faced. On the one hand, they have to be justified in terms of their relevance to a wider body of knowledge and, on the other, they have to be testable. Secondary data introduce a third consideration: how they can be tested using existing data sets.

In order to determine the strengths and limitations of official records and official statistics, a large number of questions can be asked of both types of data. With respect to official records, many of these questions will be answered in the course of gaining access to agency records, a topic discussed in a later chapter.

Perhaps because of the ease with which official statistics data can be acquired, there is a tendency to proceed directly to testing hypotheses without considering the strengths and limitations of this type of data. On the contrary, as with any research enterprise, users are required to determine the validity and reliability of data used. Specifically, a three-step process is suggested.

1. Become familiar with the documentation and major published sources examining strengths and limitations of the data source. In my experience, a major complaint of technical support people at official statistics agencies is that much of their time is wasted telling people what is clearly stated in the documentation, *if the user had only read it.*

2. Using what has been read as provisional guidelines, explore the data to determine to what extent limitations exist. For example, abrupt changes in crime trends suggest under-reporting or non-reporting. Numbers and rates that diverge substantially from other sources need further explanation. In short, generate *specific* questions about the data being used that you want to ask people who provide technical support.

3. Contact technical support people at the official statistics agencies. For example, the UCR Program in Clarksburg, West Virginia, has a number of people who are very knowledgeable and provide straightforward answers about shortcomings of the data. State

agencies and local departments will also answer questions about the data.

Doing research with secondary data is an important and economical use of the overwhelming amount of information collected about crime. While crime researchers escape some burdens associated with collecting primary data, the obligation to produce valid and reliable results remains the same. Therefore, it is as difficult and demanding to use secondary data as primary data, although the requirements for substantive use are different.

# 4

# ACCESSING AND USING OFFICIAL RECORDS

This chapter focuses on official records, which, as noted in the first chapter, are collections of statistical data that are generated as an organizational by-product of another mission or goal. Official records are found in a variety of criminal justice agencies such as police departments, detention centers, courts, treatment centers, probation departments, and prisons. This chapter describes the steps from making initial contacts for permission to use agency records through data collection and its management.

It is important to understand at the outset that agency files represent an indication of the quantity and quality of work done by the organization.

- For people being processed by the agency, the files provide an indication of their progress or status in relation to the services provided.

- For people working in the agency, the records provide an indication of the types and amounts of service given.
- For administrative staff, records make possible summary measures to supervise and evaluate service delivery.
- For the agency administrator, official records provide information to defend agency performance externally and to compete for additional resources.

Considering the importance of records, it is understandable that agency administrators develop a proprietary interest in who examines this information, the purpose of such an examination, how it is done, and the consequences of the effort. This can pose problems to crime researchers who want to utilize the records of an agency for research purposes.

Crime researchers who use official records have a unique relationship with an agency. While the information contained in agency files is essential to their research projects, the value of the research project to the agency may well be very small. Unlike a project evaluation that may be mandated and have an impact on subsequent funding, the proposed research project may have important implications for knowledge building, but have little immediate relevance to agency functioning or goals. While project evaluators are invited to use agency files, crime researchers in this case invite themselves. Despite the minimal advantage such research offers to agencies, a cursory review of journals and books suggests a high level of cooperation by agencies and a continued commitment to more and better knowledge.

The hesitation of an agency administrator to grant access to and use of agency records may be based on reasons in addition to those listed above. The administrator may display a proprietary interest in the use of files because much of the information is confidential. This includes not only the identity of people, but information related to their case. For example, while completing a research project on homicide (Riedel, Zahn, & Mock, 1985), I met with the Medical Examiner of a large U.S. city for permission to use his files on homicide. The Medical Examiner's major reservation was that, in reviewing case files, the researchers would have access to suicide cases. Some files contained suicide notes that could, if made public, be an embarrassing and humiliating intrusion into the privacy of surviving relatives.

An agency administrator may be reluctant to grant access to files because of attendant management problems. The persistent presence of another person in the agency, largely unfamiliar with the routines, formal and informal authority hierarchies, and the work values of the staff will generate conflicts and difficulties for the administrator. Further, getting the cooperation of the administrator is no guarantee that the administrator's staff will look with equal enthusiasm upon the presence of an outside person rummaging through the files.

In addition, the results of an analysis of official records may make the agency look like it is not doing an effective job. Where official records are treated as objective indicators (see Chapter 1), as occurs with many homicide studies, negative criticism of the agency may occur that is unintended by the researcher. For example, a research study comparing several cities may lead to criticisms of the agency administrator as to why his or her city has an unusually large number of robbery murders or uncleared homicides.

What may pose a somewhat greater perceived danger to the agency is an approach to official records that views the information as the product of organizational processes. Thus, research on prostitution may explain the varying arrest rates by examining changing policies and priorities determined by public opinion and political pressure on the agency administrator. Research of this type is generally done to learn the nature of organizational processes rather than to "blow the whistle" on a particular agency. However, publishing the research results makes them accessible to news and television reporters, the agency administrator's superiors, and agencies competing for the same resources that may view the results from a local and negative perspective.

Finally, an agency administrator may deny access because of having had unpleasant experiences with researchers in the past. Sometimes, such experiences stem from a researcher's view that what the agency is doing is not nearly as important as what the researcher is doing. After all, researchers are "seeking the truth," trying to find out "what is really going on"; agency people, in this view, are simply bureaucrats who are mainly concerned with holding on to their jobs. This view may be, admittedly, somewhat strained, particularly in recent decades, during which the prestige of the "scientific expert" has declined. Nonetheless, where it does exist, the agency administrator may be put in the position of constantly "putting out fires," that is, attending to a constant stream of minor and major conflicts between outside researchers and agency staff. This includes interference with work routines, staff complaints that their judgments are being questioned, personality conflicts between agency and research project staff, carelessness in protecting the confidentiality of the records, and a general lack of respect for the work values of the agency staff. In circumstances where researchers make little effort to work harmoniously with agency staff, it is not surprising that administrators will resist subsequent requests to use official records.

There are two general observations appropriate to the preceding discussion. First, projecting an image of superiority or a cynicism about the value of agency work will almost certainly doom access efforts to failure. After all, people who work in criminal justice agencies believe in the importance of their efforts and the goals of the agency. No researcher should expect agency administrators and staff to react positively to a denigration of what may be a lifetime of committed effort.

Second, crime researchers need to remember that they need the agency more than the agency needs them. Without access, there is no research project. On the other hand, the agency has been surviving in a competitive organizational milieu for some time without the benefits of the proposed research. The agency administrator is likely to believe that will continue to occur.

Good inter-personal relationships with agency personnel cannot be over-emphasized. The view taken here is that responsibility for setting and maintaining standards of behavior for the research staff belongs to the director of the research project. Not only are research directors responsible for gaining access and supervising the data collection, they are also responsible for training data collection staff in their tasks, which includes how they should interact with agency staff. During supervision, research directors also need to be alert to problems that may bring the research staff into conflict with the agency. I have attempted to make sensitivity to these issues a pervasive theme of this chapter.

## Initial Contacts

Gaining access to official records involves working simultaneously at two levels. The first level involves *tactics*. Tactics refer to any line of action, within ethical and professional limits, that has the effect of permitting the researcher to access and use agency records. Tactics involve considerations such as: Whom in the agency should be first approached for permission to use the files? How should this person be approached? What kinds of information should be given at the initial approach? Is it better to handle the approach by formal or informal means? What information about agency records should the researcher attempt to obtain at the initial stage?

The second level involves questions about the *quality of data*, which are discussed in Chapter 3. Quality of data questions turn on whether the information in agency files can meet the methodological demands of the proposed research. Is there a sufficient number of cases available in this agency to meet the requirements of statistical analysis? Can relevant operational definitions be derived from the information that is in the files? What population is reflected in agency files? Is the population serviced by the agency reasonably consistent with the population of interest in the proposed research? Is there some measure of quality control over the gathering of information that finds its way into agency files? Have there been major administrative changes that affect the collection of information?

Simultaneous consideration of tactics and quality of data is necessary because the two levels interact with one another. There is no point in gaining access to agency files if they cannot support the demands of the research. The effort to gain access can be a time-consuming and tedious process to all concerned. There is much to be lost if, after a lengthy process, the researcher finds that the records are useless for the purposes of the study.

Time and resources are lost for the researcher. For example, graduate students doing a thesis or dissertation operate under time constraints. It is disappointing and demoralizing to find, after several months of concentrated effort, that the agency files do not have sufficient validity or reliability to support the research.

Time and resources are also lost by the agency. In addition, if they have little understanding of research methods, agency administrators are not likely to appreciate a researcher who decides at the last minute not to use agency records. This is particularly true when agency administrators have had to request permission from superiors to allow use of the records and have made internal arrangements to facilitate data collection. Such an outcome may have the consequence of heightening agency resistance to future research requests.


## Finding Out Who Is in Charge

The goal of activities at this stage is to be able to interview the records manager, the person who has primary responsibility for maintaining the official records of the agency. The purpose of the contact is to evaluate the quality of agency records with a knowledgeable person to decide whether, in fact, they can support the proposed research. Getting formal permission to use the files should occur only *after* the researcher is reasonably certain the quality of official records will support the research inquiry.

Researchers who gain access to agencies for qualitative research generally agree that there is no set of tactics for gaining access that will work on all, or even most, occasions (Burgess, 1984; Johnson, 1975; Schatzman & Strauss, 1973). Sometimes, access is no more difficult than writing a letter to the agency administrator explaining the purpose of the research. In other cases, prolonged negotiation may be required.

### The Direct Approach

Where the agency has a history of cooperating with crime researchers, access can be achieved by writing a letter to the agency administrator. The letter should be on letterhead stationery and briefly describe the researcher's affiliation, the research project, records needed, and include an offer to discuss the requests further in person if desired.

This approach is most useful when there is good reason to believe it will succeed. A refusal to allow access may have the effect of "poisoning the well." In other words, if the agency administrator refuses access, subsequent efforts may be more difficult because the agency administrator now has to change his or her original decision. Unless the researcher is relatively certain that the agency administrator will react positively to the original request, it is more useful to build support for access from the bottom up.

### Using Informal Networks

Frequently, other researchers have established good working relationships with an agency and may make that network available to the newcomer. Often this takes the form of graduate students who are able to access official records with the help of a professor who has worked with the agency in the past.

When possible, it is useful for the researcher to ask other researchers about their experiences in gaining access to a particular agency. They are generally able to tell you what approaches they found successful, including the nature of negotiations with agency administrators. This is a particularly useful tactic when the agency and its environment are not familiar to the researcher. For example, in gathering information from agencies in other cities, the most useful tactic is to spend time becoming familiar with the nature of the agency by talking to other researchers who have used the agency's files. Of course, in using another person's access networks, researchers have a professional responsibility to protect its viability as if it were their own.

### Inside Informants

There is what people who do qualitative research call "the inside informant." This is a person who works within the agency of interest, is known to the researcher, and who supports the researcher's access efforts. Inside informants are primarily useful for indicating how an agency works and other people who need to be contacted. They may also be able to provide some information about the nature of the records kept by the agency.

Sometimes, however, inside informants have to be protected from themselves. They may cooperate with the researcher beyond legal and ethical bounds in, for example, showing the researcher records that are confidential. As happened to me, an inside informant indicated that no further approval was needed to collect data in the agency. Needless to say, agency administrators should be fully aware and have given permission, preferably written, to use agency files.

### Flying Blind

Determining the best person to contact in an agency can be very difficult. After reviewing the possible formal and informal approaches, the researcher may find that none are applicable. Among the least preferred approaches is one called "flying blind," simply because the probability of success is small. Nonetheless, when other options are not available, it is worth a try.

Several years ago, I was interested in doing a study of bank embez-zlement. Because this is frequently prosecuted as a federal crime, all the records of these events could be found in the federal courthouse in Philadelphia. Discussions with several people about a possible approach were unsuccessful: no one had done research using federal records.

Having concluded there was little to lose, I called the main number of the criminal prosecution division at the courthouse, explained briefly my research interests, and asked who might be the appropri-ate person to contact. Telephone staff were very helpful and, after being shunted around to two or three offices, the name of a United States Attorney was provided. I contacted him, arranged for an inter-view, and found him to be very supportive of the project and knowl-edgeable about the records.

Initial contacts are important for two reasons. First, because they are part of the agency, initial contacts have a wealth of information about the internal processes of an organization. Not only can these persons suggest how to contact the records manager, they can pro-vide an indication of general attitudes about research use of records held by the administration and the nature of problems associated with gaining access. So long as researchers make clear that they are exploring the feasibility of using official records, exploration of the preceding issues is both pertinent and relevant.

Second, because of their positions, initial contacts can provide dis-tinct perspectives on the validity of their official records. For instance, in the earlier example of using federal records to study embezzlement, a review of blank record forms with a prosecuting attorney provided insights on prosecutorial process and the quality of data.

## An Interview With the Records Manager

For researchers who do not have a long-standing relationship with an agency, the interview with the records manager is of critical importance. Not only can records managers greatly facilitate access, they can provide the most information about the quality and content of the records, short of a direct personal examination.

Because this is the first formal contact with the agency, how the researcher conducts himself or herself will be seen as indicative of the kind of person the agency will have to work with for the next few weeks or months. Whether the researcher appears to be understanding of the kinds of work done by the agency, flexible in any demands of agency time and resources, and generally cooperative will have an effect on obtaining permission to use official records. Simply put, the researcher's conduct will have a bearing on whether the records manager wants the person around and whether the records manager is willing to recommend to superiors that they allow the researcher to be around.

When interviewing the records manager about the quality of the records, it is important to remember that official records are created for administrative, not research, purposes. While information for one purpose may be made to serve another, the administrative purposes determine how and what kinds of information are gathered, how accurately and consistently the information is recorded, rules for recording it, and how it is organized and used. The reader should review the section on evaluating official records in Chapter 3 and use these as guidelines during the interview.

The interview should take place at an agreed time, preferably in the office of the records manager.

- Establish your legitimacy as a researcher by identifying the project and yourself as affiliated with a university or research agency.
- Explain the purpose and possible outcome of the anticipated research.

- Describe briefly the kinds of records needed.
- Emphasize that you are not asking formal permission to use the records, but are exploring their feasibility as a data source.
- Dress appropriately and be punctual.

It is not possible to describe in detail how the interview will progress. In the worst case, the records manager will say that the records have no value for the research project and seek to terminate the interview. In most cases, the interview process will be determined by the approach of the records manager, to which researchers should adapt themselves as much as possible. Interviews vary with directive and non-directive approaches by records managers: at one extreme are the "take charge" type of interviewers who proceed to go over the record system in detail. In this case, the researcher simply asks relevant questions as the interview proceeds. at the other end of the continuum are non-directive interviewers who expect the researcher to structure and direct the interview. In this case, the researcher should have a clear idea of what needs to be discussed, a useful order of presentation, and how far each topic needs to be pursued to learn the relevant information.

## Obtaining Formal Permission

The major question that the researcher should be able to answer at the conclusion of the interview with the records manager is whether the agency records will support the proposed inquiry. If the answer is affirmative and the records manager will lend support, then the next step is to consider how formal permission can be obtained. If the quality of the data is poor and the manager hesitant, then the researcher needs to consider alternative data sources and agencies. Finally, if the official records have sufficient quality and the records manager is hesitant, the researcher needs to address and negotiate the issues making access problematic.

There is, of course, no certainty that support of a research project by the records manager will be echoed by the agency administrator. On occasion, the head administrator may deny access despite cooperation from the staff. Generally, however, denial of access at the executive level is coupled with resistance and lack of cooperation at the level of earlier contacts.

There are two tasks that need to be accomplished between meeting with the records manager and the agency administrator. It is useful to draft a short research proposal and give it to the agency administrator prior to meeting with her.

Second, if access seems a likely outcome, it is time to review requirements for the treatment of human subjects with respect to content and time deadlines. The federal government mandates that universities review all research proposals with respect to the treatment of human subjects. Such a review and decision is made by a faculty committee that meets periodically. A researcher making the required application to satisfy Department of Health and Human Services regulations may find that the research is delayed weeks or months awaiting a committee decision. Careful attention to deadlines and meeting times can reduce the "dead time" that intervenes between application and approval.

## An Agency Research Proposal and Cover Letter

The development of an agency proposal for distribution to the executive of the agency and any involved staff is highly recommended even if it is not requested. As the research project develops in relation to the agency, minor disagreements emerge, rumors spread, and small changes in the data collection process can lead agency personnel to wonder whether the researcher is doing the research as originally verbally proposed. The presence of a written document not only increases the chances of gaining formal permission, but provides both parties with a shared background of information that can facilitate future discussions.

The agency research proposal is written exclusively to acquaint agency personnel with the proposed research. It should be two or three pages of succinct prose and should avoid technical terms or jargon. The proposal should have two sections: statement of the problem and a description of research procedures.

### Statement of the Problem

- State the purpose of the research. From the agency's perspective, how can it hope to benefit?
- Rely on a summary statement of relevant research. Avoid discussions of research literature.
- Avoid the formal language of hypotheses. State hypotheses as questions the research will answer.
- List variables in the form of information needed to answer the questions.

### Research Procedures

- Specify as accurately as possible the number and types of records needed.
- Discuss the types of comparisons that will be made to answer the research questions. Avoid a discussion of statistical techniques.
- Emphasize that data collection work routines will be arranged to minimize interference with agency work.
- Indicate that information on the records will be transcribed to a data collection form. No files will leave the agency.
- Describe steps used to maintain confidentiality.

Of course, it is always possible that the executive and/or staff people will want more detail and ask questions to that effect. The response to that issue is simple: *If* the researcher has prepared carefully to this point, the questions can be answered from available information.

The researcher may want to consider enhancing the possibility of access by an exchange. If the researcher obtains use of agency records, the agency gets some research results or evaluation it specifically wants. These additional results can take the form of collecting some additional data or providing an analysis of an issue important to the agency.

However, the researcher needs to be careful not to promise to do two research projects with the resources for one. In considering an exchange, the researcher has to consider the amount of additional work in relation to resources available.

### The Cover Letter

In addition to the agency proposal, a cover letter to the agency administrator is needed. The cover letter should describe the proposed research and records needed in one or two sentences and request a meeting to discuss permission to use the records. Of course, the letter should be typed on appropriate letterhead and show the researcher's affiliation. Included with the letter and proposal is any material related to confidentiality requirements that needs to be reviewed and agreed to by the agency. As a rule, the letter and proposal should be sent to the top administrator, such as the Police Commissioner or Director of Public Safety. It is likely that the request will be delegated to a subordinate, but that decision belongs to the agency administrator.

## The Interview With the Agency Administrator

Assuming that all goes as planned, the next step is the actual interview. It is difficult to provide guidelines for events that have a large element of unpredictability. About the only advice that can be given is: *Be prepared and expect anything!*

Sometimes, the interview may be successful and short. The agency administrator may want to do nothing more than meet the researcher and be assured that the researcher is what he or she claims to be. The "paperwork" will be turned over to a subordinate and the researcher may never see the agency administrator again. The agency administrator may even request that the entire procedure be carried out by a subordinate.

Until the time of the interview, the researcher may not know who will be present at the interview. It may be a meeting with the agency administrator alone; more frequently, one or more staff members will be present. In some cases, persons given responsibility for research and records will be present; in other cases, there will also be representatives of constituency groups affected by the research. For example, proposed research on police officers may mean that a representative of the police union will be present at the interview.

Questions and discussion can range from the simple to the complex. In any event, the level of the researcher's preparation and capacity to deal tactfully and professionally with others will be tested.

There is an assumption used in game theory that is useful here—namely, that your opponent is as intelligent as you. Any weaker assumption about the participants in the meeting is courting disaster. The researcher should be prepared to answer very penetrating questions about the nature of the research, how it will affect the routine operations of the agency, and what effects the results will have on the agency. These questions can be very difficult to answer because they can be asked not only by the agency administrator, but by members of the staff who represent very specific and important constituencies.

Unless the agency administrator has another agenda, most of the discussion will center on the contents of the proposal, cover letter, and confidentiality material. Major points relating to data access should be reviewed with the agency administrator so that there is a shared understanding; this includes the range and content of files, work routines, and confidentiality requirements.

There should be a discussion with the agency administrator about what will be done with the research once it is completed. Any plans for publication of the results should be mentioned. In many cases, agencies do not want to be identified in the research report, although this is a matter that should be discussed. As a matter of professional courtesy, the researcher should offer to supply copies of the final report to the agency.

Concerning the latter, the agency administrator or staff members may ask whether they will be able to see the results prior to the release of the final report. Put in the agency's perspective, do we get to see what the researcher is saying about us before the rest of the world sees it?

The answer to the question touches upon the issue of what the agency can expect the researcher to do if the results are perceived as highly critical of the agency's performance. There are a variety of answers to this question, but the position taken here is that the agency administrators and staff should be afforded an opportunity to read and respond to the final report prior to release or publication.

But it also should be made clear to all concerned that while the researcher is interested in the comments and criticisms that the staff may offer, the ultimate responsibility for what is contained in the final report belongs to the researcher. There are a variety of omissions, misinterpretations, and simple errors that occur in using official records that agency staff can be very helpful in correcting. Further, there may be interpretations of the results suggested that make agency performance appear less negative, which the researcher may decide have sufficient validity to incorporate within the report. However, such decisions belong exclusively to the researcher.

Finally, formal permission to use the official records requested may not be obtained at the conclusion of this meeting. For example, the agency administrator may agree to using certain kinds of official records, but not others. There are two general suggestions that need to be briefly mentioned. First, the lines of communication need to be kept open. It should be understood that while the researcher cannot immediately agree to the restrictions requested, he or she would like to pursue the matter in a subsequent meeting. Second, the researcher needs to evaluate the requested restrictions in terms of the integrity of the proposed research. What is the impact of the restrictions on the measurement of important variables, the rigor of the research design, and the generalizability of the results? If the researcher cannot tolerate restrictions under any circumstances, the project must be abandoned. On the other hand, there are a variety of ways to negotiate obstacles between the researcher and the agency that will meet the interests of both parties.

## The Data Collection Process

The role demands on the researcher shift in this stage from being a person interested in access to one interested in implementation and maintenance. This includes data collection, management of the collection process, relationships among the research staff, and relationships with agency staff. The following discussion assumes that data are collected from paper files rather than supplied from computer media by the agency.

### Building Trust Relationships

It is essential to develop relationships of trust between the researcher and the research staff, and with agency staff. To some extent, the researcher has developed a reputation for trustworthiness in the process of gaining access or she or he would not be there. It does not follow, however, that agency staff view the researcher's staff in the same way.

Field researchers also face problems of establishing trust. Emerson (1983) and Schatzman and Strauss (1973) suggest that agency staff not only want to know what researchers (observers) and their staff are up to, but also whether or not they are trustworthy. Specifically, Johnson (1983) notes:

> In this respect, the observer's personal characteristics will be combined in a variety of ways to make imputations of motive, intention, and purpose to evaluate moral character. Numerous putative traits such as one's sexual status, racial status, socioeconomic background, educational background, and personal biography may be used to make such determinations. Furthermore, these are combined with other common-sense cultural understandings about the observer's deference, demeanor, and presentation of himself as evaluations of moral character and trustworthiness are made. (pp. 112-113)

Trust relationships are important if data collection is to proceed smoothly. There are a multitude of occasions where it is necessary for research staff to interact with agency people. These occasions include locating missing files, deciphering abbreviations and acronyms in files, borrowing pencils, finding out about the best public transportation routes, and even getting help in finding the coffee or soda machine. Where good relationships prevail between staff and researchers, these simple matters pose no problems.

There is a series of tasks facing the researcher prior to and during the actual data collection. They are

- Developing a work routine for the staff
- Developing a data collection form and codebook
- Pre-testing the data collection form and codebook
- Selection and training of staff
- General orientation and site training
- Management and quality control

## Developing a Work Routine

Prior to the actual data collection, a second meeting should be scheduled with the records manager to articulate the data collection process with agency routines. The following items need to be addressed:

- Providing the records manager with an estimate of the total amount of time needed to collect data from official records
- Negotiating a daily and weekly timetable for data collection so that data collection is not occurring during peak times of agency use of records
- Determining the procedure to be followed by data collection staff in drawing and refiling dossiers so the routine work of the agency is not hampered
- Determining the contact person able to resolve questions about unclear or ambiguous entries in the files
- Arranging for work space for the data collection staff
- Arranging for storage space of completed and blank data collection forms
- Discussing security concerns such as identification badges and staff transportation to and from the site, especially in high-crime areas

## Developing a Data Collection Form and Codebook

The next step is to develop a data collection form and an accompanying codebook. Unless the researcher is planning to gather the data without help, it is useful to begin working with no more than one or two staff members.

A data collection form is a paper-and-pencil schedule on which file information is organized into cases, variables, and attributes or values. Each value of a variable is assigned machine-readable elements or numbers called codes. For example, the gender of an offender is coded "1" for males and "2" for females. An accompanying codebook is an instruction and translation device: It shows the data collector and subsequent users what the codes mean and how each of the values of a variable is coded.

There are a number of sources that provide detailed information on how to construct data collection forms and codebooks. Research methods texts typically include a chapter on data collection techniques. Both Smith (1991) and Bailey (1994a) provide particularly useful chapters on preparing data for computer analysis.

Another source is colleagues or researchers, who typically are quite willing to supply copies of their data collection forms and codebooks. An examination of the literature review will provide names of researchers who have done inquiries in the same area. The latter can be contacted and copies of their data collection forms and codebooks obtained.

Carolyn Rebecca Block and Richard Block (1997) have gathered data on all homicides reported to the Chicago Police Department from 1965 through 1995. They have prepared a detailed codebook and coding instructions that are available on the Internet at: *http://www.icpsr.umich.edu/NACJD/archive.html.*

Very early in the data collection process, the researcher should contact the computer center where the data will be processed. Staff members can frequently suggest a variety of methods for preparing the data for computer analysis. In addition, computer center staff will alert the researcher that how data are collected, codes assigned, and data entered are not entirely independent of the statistical techniques used for analysis. As a rule, statistical packages such as SPSS or SAS have standard input formats and provide a large array of statistical techniques. Where the researcher is planning to use a technique that is not part of frequently used packages, it is important to explore with computer center staff how data can be collected to satisfy the input demands of the technique.

The next step in developing a data collection form and codebook is to visit the agency and draw a typical sample of 10 or 20 dossiers from recent years. Ideally, these dossiers should contain all the information collected because they will shape the data collection form and codebook. The following are some general guidelines:

- A data collection form should be designed to involve a minimum of interpretation of file information. Where interpretation of file information is required, the codebook should provide explicit coding instructions for codes and variables.

- Personal identifiers, such as names, should not appear on a data collection form because they pose a persistent and unnecessary confidentiality risk. Develop a system of numerical identifiers for the data set at the outset.

- Code major numerical identifiers used in the agency. This is useful if data collectors need to return to the files to rectify an error discovered at a later stage of the data collection.

- Where personal identifiers are needed to match files at some other agency, one master list can be kept by the researcher.

- The data collection form should be developed in a way that meshes with the organization of agency records. Ideally, data collectors should be able to take a dossier and follow it in a page-by-page fashion in completing a data collection form. Where the data collector has to consult separate files, items from these files should be clustered together on the data collection form so that all information can be recorded in one step.

- Establish a definite beginning and ending point for the data set. The codebook should operationally define the time period covered by the data set. Not only is that necessary information for coders, but it makes later description of the data set much clearer.

- In developing a data collection form and collecting data, begin with the most recent period and work backward. Forms tend to become more detailed as years pass. Developing a data collection form from dossiers at the beginning date of the data set runs the risk of having to reconstruct the data collection form if new and useful information is added later to agency forms. When this reconstruction occurs during the process of data collection, the researcher may be faced with the task of recoding information already collected.

- The data collection form should be designed to collect data at the lowest feasible level of abstraction. Statistical packages provide an endless variety of methods to aggregate detailed data, so classification schemes should be postponed to the analysis stage. Because classification, by definition, loses detail, the researcher may be imposing unnecessary restrictions on the analysis.

- Collect as much information as feasible. While the preceding guideline has to do with the level of specificity, the present one focuses on what kinds of information should be collected that are *apparently* not relevant to the research. File information can range from the essential to the clearly not relevant. It is in the midrange of such a dimension that questions are posed for the development of the data collection form. The rule of thumb suggested is that if it *may* be needed, it should be collected to avoid the large costs associated with obtaining it later.

- A series of missing codes should be developed. What will be defined as the codes for missing information needs to be specified in the data collection form and codebook. It is convenient to use the same digits as missing codes throughout the form. Consider whether separate codes are needed to reflect different reasons for missing data.

## Pre-Testing the Data Collection Form and Codebook

Pre-testing can be done by drawing 10 or 15 new dossiers from the file and coding them. It is preferable to have someone do the coding who has not played a major role in the development of the data collection form and codebook. This type of coder is useful because he can approach the task with a fresh view and is more likely to make the researcher aware of errors, misunderstandings, and confusing instructions. To ensure reliability, the researcher and a staff member should recode the same 10 or 15 dossiers and compare their results to the pre-test coding.

The data from the 10 or 15 completed data collection forms also should be entered in a computer file. This gives the researcher an opportunity to determine what kinds of difficulties will be encountered entering the data into the computer prior to the actual beginning of the data collection. Once this is completed, the changes can be incorporated into the final version of the data collection form and codebook.

## Selection and Training of Staff

To a limited extent, selection and training have already occurred. Where the researcher is working with one or two staff members in developing the data collection form and codebook, those individuals are familiar with the proposed research and are a familiar sight in the agency. The researcher should capitalize on the experience of this staff and ask them to help develop the procedures for selecting and training additional staff.

The first step is the development and implementation of a recruitment plan for additional staff. This plan includes a specification of the number of people needed, description of the positions, periods of employment, duties of the positions, salaries, and advertising.

Selecting staff members is a critically important task for the researcher. Sometimes it is useful to have the one or two current staff members participate in the selection interview. Picking people who have the research skills and availability to remain with the project throughout the period of data collection is essential, but that is the least difficult task.

The most difficult task is selecting staff who will interact well with agency staff and contribute to a building of trust relationships with the agency. During interviews with applicants, the researcher should explain the type of work to be done, the nature of the setting, and specific expectations. Also, the researcher should ascertain whether the interviewees have any problems, personal or otherwise, working with the kinds of people they will encounter in the agency. People with extreme or highly biased views about certain types of agency personnel, such as a negative bias toward police officers, should be avoided. After selection is completed, the next step is training the staff.

## General Orientation and Site Training

There are several issues that need to be covered prior to sending additional staff members to an agency. These include the following:

- Determine that all staff members have gone through the proper bureaucratic channels to ensure they will be paid regularly.
- Identify staff working hours and supervisors.
- Provide staff members with data collection forms and codebooks. Ask them to review them prior to site training.
- Emphasize the importance of maintaining good relationships with agency staff.
- Review confidentiality requirements. Emphasize that agency files and collection forms remain in the agency. Information in agency files should not be discussed outside the work setting.
- Review security arrangements. Explain the requirement for wearing identification badges.
- Discuss safe transportation to and from the work site, if needed.
- Assign a numerical identifier to each staff member. Explain the need to code these and how they will be used to maintain quality control.

### Site Training

Site training refers to teaching the staff members to use the data collection forms and codebook by coding information from agency files. Each data collector should be given an agency file and "walked through" the dossier and each item of the data collection form. Because there are likely to be many questions at this point, the researcher should have the original one or two staff members present to help answer them. The coding of the first few cases will be very slow, with numerous questions and much consulting of the code-book. As the data collectors code more cases, they begin to remember the various codes and the entire process moves faster.

The researcher should encourage an informal chain of command. Questions about files and coding should first be referred to the more experienced staff member. If that person cannot answer the question, the two staff members should consult the agency staff member assigned by the records manager. This procedure reserves for agency staff only those questions that cannot be answered in other ways.

After each new staff member has coded two or three cases, the same cases should be recoded by a more experienced staff member and the results compared. This method will serve to bring any errors or misunderstandings of instructions to light before the new staff member introduces the error into subsequent cases.

The research staff should be informed that no completed forms leave the agency without a supervisor's awareness. Replacing completed data collection forms that have been lost represents an expenditure of resources and a possible disruption of the data collection process. Research staff should be told where the blank and completed forms can be stored in the agency between coding sessions.

It is important to inform research staff that, after they have completed coding a case, dossiers are to be refiled in exactly the fashion in which they were found. Nothing frustrates agency personnel more than not being able to find a file when needed, and subsequently discovering that it has been misfiled or mislaid by careless research staff.

As more cases are coded and new staff become more proficient, the attention of the researcher needs to be given over to activities that maintain the data collection process and bring it to a successful termination.

## Management and Quality Control

Once the data collection process begins to move smoothly, the researcher needs to implement a system of quality control. One approach is to have a randomly selected case of a staff member recoded by more experienced coders and the results compared. As new staff become more proficient, they may recode a case drawn from another staff member's work. This process should be done at least once a week, probably more often in the early stages of data collection.

The person doing the recoding should make a record of disagreements between the two coding efforts. This should be made available to the researcher, who reviews them to determine the source of the difficulties and what corrections have been made.

The researcher needs to coordinate the efforts of the data collectors with persons responsible for entering the data into the computer. It is preferable to have the data entered into the computer as soon as possible for two reasons. Obviously, the more quickly data are entered, the more rapidly analysis can begin. In addition, a program of regular data entry creates another copy so that any unexpected event that leads to destruction of data collection forms reduces the amount of loss to the research project.

It is also necessary to specify the transportation link for data forms between the agency and computer processing site. The researcher should designate the person responsible for transporting the forms and how often it should be done. When forms are being transported from a remote location, the researcher has to devise secure methods of transportation. In devising such methods, the researcher may have to balance the costs of some relatively expensive, but secure, forms of transportation against the cost, as well as the delay, of reacquiring the data. As a result of such a comparison, an apparently expensive form of transportation may turn out to be very inexpensive indeed.

The researcher needs to monitor the nature of the interaction between research and agency staff. In going about their daily duties, agency staff will be curious about the nature of the research. They will, as a matter of course, strike up conversations with research staff members to learn what is going on in their domain. If the researcher has been straightforward about the nature of the project, research staff explanations will coincide with what agency staff members may already know. Once the curiosity of the agency staff member is satisfied, work will typically continue without any difficulties.

The researcher needs to be aware that conflicts between research and agency staff can emerge from a wide variety of causes. This can occur despite the best efforts of the researcher, the research staff, and agency administrators to create trust and cooperation. Where a serious conflict seems to be emerging, the researcher should arrange to discuss the matter with the records manager and, if necessary, with the agency administrator. If the researcher is successful in defining the conflict as a problem shared by the agency and the research team, rather than one belonging to one or the other, it is more likely that a successful resolution of the issue will be found.

The researcher also needs to monitor the behavior and morale of the research staff. There may be personality conflicts among research staff members that can be minimized by having different individuals work together. Occasionally, as happened on a project of mine, everyone who tried to work with one particular staff member eventually refused to do so: the person became a social isolate. When this occurs, it may be necessary to reassign that person to other duties where there is little contact with the research staff, such as preparing data for computer input.

Sometimes the nature of the data collection may have detrimental effects on research staff's functioning and morale. For example, collecting data on homicide cases can be very depressing work. In the case of a homicide research project I was involved in, full-time data collection from the files of police departments and medical examiners was having negative psychological effects (Riedel, Zahn, & Mock, 1985). One reason was that medical examiners routinely keep in their files very detailed photographs of the victim's injuries. Viewing pictures and detailed descriptions of human slaughter day after day led to staff complaints of sleeplessness, persistent nightmares, and sleep-walking, preceded by large amounts of alcohol consumption at the end of each workday. A decision to reduce the workday from 8 to 6 hours substantially reduced the problems.

At the conclusion of the data collection stage, the researcher should meet one more time with the records manager to express appreciation for the cooperation. In addition, the researcher should indicate that, while data collection is mostly complete, the researcher or a staff member may have to return to correct minor errors in the coding. It is important for the researcher to indicate that such occasional visits, particularly by staff members, will be preceded by phone calls from the researcher to the records manager. This step is necessary, not only to coordinate time periods when the relevant people are available, but also to prevent unauthorized access to the records.

## A Final Note

This chapter has focused on gaining access to and using agency records for research purposes. Throughout, I have emphasized the dual themes of building working relationships with agency personnel in the process of requesting and using their files for research purposes.

There are two issues that have been discussed in previous chapters and bear on the problems of access and use. First, it is extremely important that the researcher have a firm grasp of the research literature, especially in the early stages of access. Nothing undermines researchers' credibility faster than giving the impression that they do not know what they are talking about.

Second, I recommend a review of the sections in Chapter 3 describing guidelines for evaluating official records. While they are not an exhaustive list of questions, they should be part of the interview with the records manager.

# 5

# METHODOLOGICAL ISSUES

Three issues central to the use of secondary data are discussed in this chapter. They are classification, missing data, and linkages between and within reporting systems. The trend of the discussion moves from an issue that affects both primary and secondary data (classification) to one that is peculiar to secondary data (linkages). Missing data are a problem for all types of data, but secondary data present a unique configuration.

## The Nature of Classification

Classification is the process of ordering objects into classes or categories on the basis of their relationships (May, 1982). For example, males and females are different classes that share a relationship of sexual orientation or gender. Catholic, Jewish, and Protestant are different classes sharing a relationship of religious preferences.

Simple classification requires that the classes formed are exhaustive and mutually exclusive. This means that each and every object must fit into one of the classes (exhaustive), and a given object cannot be classified into more than one class (mutually exclusive). While this is a simple matter with respect to variables like gender, it becomes more problematic for statistical analyses when there are a large number of objects with small frequencies. For example, weapons can be classified into handguns; long guns; cutting and stabbing instruments; blunt instruments such as clubs; and personal weapons such as hands, feet, and teeth. But what can be done with more exotic choices like pellet guns, ropes, garrotes, and poisons? Typically, where the frequencies are small, these weapons as classified as "other," which preserves the requirements of classification.

Classification is necessary to measurement or assigning of numbers to classes. The task of assigning numbers to classes, or mapping, presumes a classification of objects: For example, males can be given a value of "2" while females are assigned "1." In this instance, gender is described as a nominal level of measurement, which is basically the assignment of numbers to classes.

There are three higher levels (ordinal, interval, and ratio) that impose additional measuring requirements, but all levels require classification. Drawing on an original paper by S. S. Stevens (1951), virtually all criminal justice and criminology texts describe the four levels of measurement.

## Classification Is Purposeful Activity

Classification is purposeful activity reflecting theory, previous research, present research, policy, and/or practice. The relevance of purpose for classification is described by Bailey (1994b):

> Imagine that we throw a mixture of 30 knives, forks, and spoons into a pile on a table and ask three people to group them by "similarity." Imagine our surprise when three different classifications result. One person classifies into two groups of utensils, the long and the short.

> Another classifies into three classes—plastic, wooden, and silver. The
> third person classifies into three groups—knives, forks, and spoons.
> Whose classification is "best"? (p. 2)

The answer, of course, depends on the purpose of the classification.
Are the utensils to be classified by size, composition, or use for eat-
ing? To take a more familiar example, library books are classified by
subject area rather color of the cover or book weight because the purpose is to make them accessible to patrons looking for books on specific subjects.

Are there classifications in crime research that have a high degree
of consensus? Such settled classifications are sometimes called
"natural" classifications. Simon (1969) defines natural classifications
as those that are used for many different purposes, while artificial
classifications are constructed for specific research purposes.

It's difficult to find any classification in the literature on crime for
which there is sufficient widespread consensus or settled use to qualify as a natural classification. Consider the simple task of classifying
violent crimes. Typically, these include homicide, rape, robbery, and
aggravated assault. Yet, a staff report for a Presidential Commission
on Violence defined criminal violence to include disorderly conduct,
burglary, and vandalism (Mulvihill & Tumin, 1969). The authors of
the report argued "that property harm cannot be separated from the
inconvenience, discomfort, or suffering" of the property owner. The
"elderly lady whose apartment is burglarized, severely damaged,
and left in a state of disarray may experience psychological trauma
and considerable physical discomfort before her personal property is
repaired and replaced" (p. 5).

According to Bailey (1994b), classification is criticized as being
descriptive, pre-explanatory, or non-explanatory. There are two
responses to the criticisms that classification is "merely descriptive"
and fails to meet the goal of explanation. First, classification is a fundamental task of science because classification is a foundation for

explanation. It is not possible to explain the differences between apples and oranges unless they are first described as objects (Bailey, 1994b).

Second, Hood and Sparks (1970) have argued that rather than theory presupposing classification, it is the reverse: Classification presupposes theory. Typologies cannot be developed, they assert, without a guiding theory to indicate which types should be included. It is difficult to say whether all classification must involve formal theory, but it is clear that classification, as purposeful activity, must involve conceptualization. As conceptual activity, classification can be viewed as statements describing phenomena at a lower level of abstraction than those used for explanation.

### Advantages of Classification

Classification is useful to reduce the complexity of phenomena and to explore similarities and differences. Bailey (1994b) discusses several other advantages, as well as disadvantages, but the discussion here will be limited to the ones mentioned.

Because researchers cannot focus on all people and characteristics at once, classification reduces the relevant dimensions to a size that can be managed for analysis. But the reduction of complexity is achieved at the cost of the loss of the individuality of observations. For example, because Latinos or Hispanics are an ethnic and not a racial group, homicide data from the National Center of Health Statistics classified them as "white" until 1984 (Riedel, 1999).

Classification facilitates identification of similarities and differences. For example, suppose a researcher is interested in exploring relationships between weapons and type of homicide and is faced with the task of classifying stabbing instruments. By a careful examination of the data, it becomes clear that there are no important relationships among the variety of stabbing instruments and type of homicide. It makes no difference whether the stabbing instrument is a table knife, fork, paring knife, carving knife, bread knife, or butcher knife. However, by grouping this variety of knives in one class, the researcher finds a relationship between weapons and homicides such that stabbing instruments are frequently used by female intimate partner offenders against male victims (Riedel & Best, 1998). Considering that intimate partner homicides occur in private settings that have kitchens and are usually the outcome of a highly emotional argument between intimate partners, it is easy to see that in the heat of the moment, the female intimate partner grabs whatever weapon is handy—which will probably be a knife of some sort—and stabs her male partner.

Supposing, on the other hand, there is a difference among types of stabbing instruments and homicides. Suppose, for example, that the variety of stabbing instruments found in kitchens has a different relationship to homicides by comparison to stilettos, hunting knives, machetes, bayonets, sabers, and switchblades? In that instance, the classification is refined to include sub-types of stabbing instruments that are then compared to homicides.

## Classification and Secondary Data

Like researchers using primary data, researchers using secondary data have the opportunity to classify phenomena based on hypotheses, previous theories, and research. Unlike researchers using primary data, secondary researchers use data rife with classifications because these data are information collected for another purpose. Therefore, the challenge for secondary data users is to develop theoretically relevant and methodologically sound classifications from information on crime classified along a variety of other dimensions.

From one historically important perspective, classification is the *sine qua non* of criminology. In discussing a sociological and scientific approach to the study of crime, Sellin (1938) writes,

The unqualified acceptance of the legal definitions of the basic units or elements of criminological inquiry violates a fundamental criterion of science. The scientist must have freedom to define his own terms, based on the intrinsic character of his material and designating properties in that material which are assumed to be universal. . . . It should be emphasized at this point that the above comments do not imply that the criminal law or the data about crimes and criminals assembled in the process of its enforcement are not useful in scientific research. They are indeed a rich source for the scientist, but the application of scientific criteria to the selection and classification of these data independently of their *legal* form is essential to render them valuable to science. . . . The data of the criminal law and the data about crimes and criminals now subservient to legal categories must be "processed" by the scientist before he can use them. (italics in the original; pp. 23-25)

Contemporary researchers refer to the "processing" suggested by Sellin as disaggregating data. Flewelling and Williams (1999) provide a thoughtful discussion of the need to develop a typology of homicide that would be useful across a wide range of research questions and theoretical perspectives. The two objectives that would be achieved by a relevant classification of homicide are applicable to a wide range of research with secondary data.

First, a classification system helps to establish correlational and ostensibly causal relationships between causal, or independent variables, and effects, or dependent variables. Pertinent variables may be either individual-level, cultural, or social structural variables.

Crime rates show variation in the amount of crime over time or across jurisdictions. But a decline in the rate of a particular crime may represent a change in the mixes of crimes that are occurring. Without an adequate classification of types, such a result would be missed. For example, it has been noted previously that clearance by arrest rates for homicide has declined from approximately 90% to about two thirds of homicides reported since 1961. Is the decline due to less efficient policing or is it due to the decline in family-related murders, which are easier to clear by arrest than felony-related homicides (Riedel & Jarvis, 1998)?

Second, public awareness, prevention strategies, and policy options are shaped to some extent by empirical data. Well-developed classifications are useful in defining high-risk groups and types of homicide that are most prevalent. Where there is consensus about these classifications, they can serve as a basis for prevention strategies as well as an avenue of public awareness (Flewelling & Williams, 1999).

## Some Instances of Disaggregating Secondary Data

Preceding paragraphs have argued that classification is purposeful and that the use of secondary data for crime research requires "processing" or disaggregating of data. In this final part of the section, some instances are given of how secondary data are reclassified for criminological purposes.

### *Disaggregation Can Be Theoretically Driven*

Drawing on the routine activities perspective (Cohen & Felson, 1979; Felson & Cohen, 1980), Sherman, Gartin, and Buerger (1989) have argued that the most appropriate unit of analysis for an ecological theory is place. To explore the relevance of places, the authors drew upon centralized police dispatching systems that provide precise locations for police calls for services. Comparing addresses for service calls with an estimate of total Minneapolis addresses led Sherman et al. to reclassify locations in terms of their criminal activity.

The authors found that relatively few places, or "hot spots," received a large percentage of all police calls. Slightly more than half (50.4%) of all calls to the police for which cars were dispatched went to 3.3% of addresses. In turn, these results offer several possibilities for crime reduction, ranging from increased patrol of certain places to making hot spots less attractive targets. For example, convenience stores can be required to have two or more clerks on duty to increase guardianship.

## Exploring the Homogeneity of a Classification Category

Methodologically, classification requires there be more important differences between classes than within them. One instance of where classes will have to be refined involves race and ethnicity.

Much crime research, especially violence research, has focused on the distinction between whites and African Americans. Hawkins (1999) argues persuasively that it is time to move beyond simple black-white comparisons. He points to a number of findings that are the result of disaggregation:

- There are substantial regional differences in homicide among African Americans.
- There are large variations in African American homicides attributable to socioeconomic differentiation within the Black community.
- There are variations in African American homicides not only across cities, but in areas within cities.

Hawkins (1999) is undoubtedly correct in pointing out that in recent decades the United States has become more ethnically and racially diverse. Generally, whites and African Americans remain as two distinct racial classes, but Hispanics and Latinos are becoming a larger proportion of the population and, because many are disadvantaged, they contribute to statistics on crime. Increasingly, therefore, secondary data have had to distinguish race and ethnicity. What complicates the classification of Hispanics even further is whether they should be further differentiated into regions of origin: Mexico, Central America, Latin America, and Puerto Rico (Moore & Pinderhughes, 1993).

Similarly, a variety of Asian/Pacific Islanders are found in crime data as victims and/or offenders in some areas of the United States. In California homicide data, for example, Asian/Pacific Islanders include 14 different classes of national or cultural origin (Riedel, 1998).

While official records and official statistics have modified their classifications, crime researchers have done little research on the diverse ethnic groups that are appearing in crime data. Hispanics are the most obvious recent ethnic group, yet the research on crime involving Hispanics is limited, focusing predominantly on gangs (Klein, Maxson, & Miller, 1995) and violence (Block, 1993; Kraus, Sorenson, & Juarez, 1988; Martinez, 1997).

There is an excessive reliance on the simple African American and white distinction in research. As Hawkins (1999) notes, "there is no clear theoretical basis to expect that race is a more significant predictor of group differences in homicide than ethnicity, SES [socioeconomic status], place of residence, and similar attributes of offenders and victims and the environments in which they live" (p. 199).

As more research and theory become available, relationships between crime patterns and relevant classifications of race and ethnicity will become better known. For example, can Mexican Americans be combined with Puerto Ricans or Central Americans to form a homogeneous category of Hispanics or Latinos? A partial answer depends on the theoretical importance of a distinction between different ethnic and racial groups. Another way of resolving the problem is to examine the relationships of different racial/ethnic groups to other important variables.

### Reclassification for
### Methodological and Statistical Reasons

Variables found in secondary data are frequently classified to meet methodological and statistical requirements. As noted earlier, cases are classified under the heading of "other" where they cannot be combined into a theoretically relevant class, are too few to be analyzed separately, or both.

Earlier it was noted that classification leads to the loss of the individuality of cases. That may be desirable when the validity of the data is in doubt. For example, suppose in recording age of offenders from police records there are independent indications that reported age is not recorded accurately. Is it necessary to discard the information completely?

As Chapter 4 indicates, age and similar information should be *collected* in as detailed a manner as is feasible. However, in preparation for *analysis*, the age variable can be classified in wide intervals up to and including a dichotomy based on a central value. While collapsing data categories minimizes error, it discards large amounts of specific data. But because what is discarded may not be valid, crude reclassification may provide information not available if the variable is discarded entirely.

## Missing Data

In social science research, missing information can lead to a variety of incomplete and misleading results. Missing data have a different configuration in research using official records and statistics in comparison to survey research. First, a survey researcher either mails a carefully constructed questionnaire to a sample of respondents or sends trained interviewers to query people about issues that are less emotionally immediate than crime victimization. As was noted in Chapter 1, crime victims are emotionally upset, and the data recorders vary widely in their experience and commitment to accurate records. The problem is further compounded by major participants (offenders) who try to avoid giving any information at all!

Second, some survey respondents cannot be contacted despite repeated attempts. Crime researchers are limited to reported crime and have only the vaguest idea of the number of criminal acts and actors. While the survey researcher knows the extent of "unit non-responses," the crime researcher can only guess at the number of "missing cases," based on previous self-report studies.

Finally, survey researchers have a problem of "item or question non-responses," usually centered on the frequently understandable reluctance of respondents to provide specific pieces of information such as income. Crime researchers find "missing values" scattered throughout official records and statistics with no apparent patterns.

Crime researchers, for the most part, have done little to cope with the problem of missing data, being satisfied to use what is available and ignore what is not. Because there is little specific information available about how data might be weighted to account for unreported crime, this section will focus on the unavailability of information in records, that is, missing values.

*Missing data* is the general term; it refers to "missing cases" and "missing values." As Babbie (1986) notes, cases can be individuals, groups, or social artifacts. Cases are units used for the "ultimate purpose of aggregating their characteristics in order to describe some larger group or explain some abstract phenomena" (p. 74). Missing cases exist when alternate sources show that all the relevant instances are not recorded. For example, observation of patrol behavior as well as National Crime Victimization Survey (NCVS) reports indicate that not all incidents of domestic violence are reported.

*Values* are characteristics describing objects, and *variables* are logical groupings of values. Thus, "male" and "female" are values and "gender" is a variable. Where variables are mapped onto a number system, it must be possible to assign at least two values, that is, variables must vary. The assignment can be as simple as "1" for the presence of a characteristic and "0" for its absence.

But note that assigning a number for the absence of an attribute is not the same as a missing value. Assigning a value for the absence of an attribute reflects a positive state of knowledge: The case *does not* have the value "a" for variable $X_1$. *Missing values reflect a state of ignorance: We do not know what the value is.* For example, offender data will sometimes leave blank the space for "prior criminal record." Does this mean the offender had no prior criminal record, or that the

**TABLE 5.1**  Data Matrix

| Cases | Y | $X_1$ | $X_2$ | Variables $X_3$ | $X_4$ | $X_5$ | $X_6$ |
|-------|---|-------|-------|-------|-------|-------|-------|
| 1 | 0 | 1 | 1 | 1 | 1 | 1 | 1 |
| 2 | 1 | 0 | 1 | 1 | 1 | 1 | 1 |
| 3 | 1 | 1 | 0 | 1 | 1 | 1 | 1 |
| 4 | 1 | 1 | 1 | 0 | 1 | 1 | 1 |
| 5 | 1 | 1 | 1 | 1 | 0 | 1 | 1 |
| 6 | 1 | 1 | 1 | 1 | 1 | 0 | 1 |
| 7 | 1 | 1 | 1 | 1 | 1 | 1 | 0 |

Y = Dependent Variable; X = Independent Variable; 1 = Reported Value; 0 = Missing Value

recorder did not know anything about the offender's prior criminal history?

There are ways that crime researchers handle missing data in secondary analysis. Listwise, pairwise, and mean substitution are three common methods. A brief description of each follows.

## Listwise and Pairwise Deletion

One strategy is to ignore missing data when conducting analysis. To do so, crime researchers employ listwise or pairwise deletion. Listwise deletion occurs where cases with *any* missing values are dropped from further analysis. An example illustrates these techniques.

Table 5.1 is a hypothetical data matrix of seven cases, one dependent variable (Y), and six independent variables ($X_1$ through $X_6$). Each one of the variables has only one missing value. Suppose the crime researcher decides to use a multivariate statistical technique, that is, a statistic that uses all the independent variables ($X_1$ through $X_6$) to determine their relative importance in explaining the dependent variable (Y). A requirement of these techniques is that the values for each variable and each case are completely reported. If there are one or more missing values, the entire case is dropped from the analysis. Inspection of Table 5.1 indicates that listwise deletion leaves the researcher with no cases to analyze; that is, all cases are dropped from the analysis because there are no complete cases.

Suppose, on the other hand, that the researcher decides to use a bivariate statistical technique; that is, he or she compares the dependent variable with one independent variable at a time. Thus, a statistical test would compare Y to $X_1$, then compare Y to $X_2$, Y to $X_3$, and so on.

This makes a critical difference in terms of missing cases. Where Y is compared to $X_1$, only two cases are dropped from the analysis because of missing values (see Table 5.1). The latter is pairwise deletion, but it would be a gain over listwise deletion because only two cases would be lost rather than all of them.

Pairwise deletion poses a different sort of problem. Table 5.1 indicates that a comparison of Y and $X_1$ would use a different subset of cases from Y and $X_2$. In the first comparison (Y and $X_1$), cases 1 and 2 would be excluded; in the second (Y and $X_2$), cases 1 and 3 would be eliminated from the analysis.

If crime researchers assume that the data are drawn from the same population and that the results of bivariate tests with different independent variables can be compared to one another, they may be in error. Comparisons are, in fact, made on samples drawn from overlapping populations. In addition, pairwise deletion can create statistical anomalies (Cohen & Cohen, 1983).

## Mean Substitution

The most widely used method of eliminating missing values, first suggested by Wilks (1932), is mean substitution. The purpose is to restore the sample to its original size by substituting the mean of the distribution of known values for missing values. But mean substitution has the unfortunate consequence of unduly reducing the variability of the distribution.

Researchers frequently compute the arithmetical mean as well as a measure of how much the values in the distribution scatter around the mean. While the meaning of arithmetical means is known, the essential idea behind measures of variability (mean deviations, standard deviations, and variances) can be understood by considering the relevant conceptual component. Without getting into the specifics of computing each of the three measures, each value in the distribution is subtracted from the mean, then the resulting differences (or deviations) are summed and divided by the number of cases. It is not difficult to imagine that if the mean value is substituted for missing values, the deviations will be zero for those values although the number of cases with non-missing values has now increased. Hence, variability is reduced.

To illustrate the effect of mean substitution, random samples of 100 cases and 500 cases were selected from 3,018 of 3,061 homicides reported to the California Criminal Justice Statistics Center in 1996 (Riedel, 1998). In order to have a completely reported variable, 43 cases with missing values on victim's age were deleted. To simulate missing data, different percentages of values for victims' age were randomly deleted. For example, after calculating a mean and variance (a measure of variability) for 100 cases, 5% of cases were randomly deleted, the mean of the reduced sample was inserted in place of the missing values, and then the mean and variance of the reconstituted distribution were calculated. The same steps were followed in deleting 10%, 20%, and 30% of the 100-case distribution, and the procedure was repeated on the sample of 500 cases. The results are given in Table 5.2.

Table 5.2 shows that the mean ages for homicide victims remain virtually unchanged while the measure of variability decreases by a substantial amount. The variance is 253.9 for 100 cases and 222.6 for 500 cases when no values are missing, but as means are substituted

**TABLE 5.2** Effect on the Mean and Variance of Mean Substitution for Different Sample Sizes and Percentages of Missing Values

|  | *None* *Missing* | *5%* *Missing* | *10%* *Missing* | *20%* *Missing* | *30%* *Missing* |
|---|---|---|---|---|---|
| Mean | 31.2 | 31.2 | 31.7 | 30.7 | 30.3 |
| Variance | 253.9 | 251.8 | 222.9 | 194.0 | 162.3 |
| N | 100 | 100 | 100 | 100 | 100 |
| Mean | 30.0 | 30.1 | 30.3 | 30.3 | 29.5 |
| Variance | 222.6 | 216.7 | 195.2 | 176.9 | 150.1 |
| N | 500 | 500 | 500 | 500 | 500 |

for an increasingly large number of missing values, the variance declines. Put another way, mean substitution will produce the least distortion if the percentage of missing values is small and a substantially greater distorting effect as the percentage of missing values increases. Because both mean and variance are essential components in a wide variety of statistical tests, mean substitution will have a marked negative effect on resulting analyses.

## Good News and Bad News

The good news is that in some studies missing values may not have a biasing effect on comparisons. The bad news is that this is unlikely to happen with crime-related data.

Suppose there are 100 cases of police-recorded homicides that contain demographic and event-related information for both victims and offenders. For 35 of these cases, the official records indicate no offender has been arrested, that is, the offense has not been "cleared by arrest." Hence, these cases are missing offender-related information and therefore are missing values for victim-offender relationships and offender's age, race, and gender, although similar victim variables are fully recorded.

The question is whether information on victim variables can be used only for those cases where offender information is available or whether a researcher should assume that victims whose offenders have not been arrested are significantly different from those whose offenders are arrested. Does the value of victim's age, for example, depend upon whether the offense is cleared?

To determine the answer, victim variables for two groups, cleared and uncleared, need to be compared. If statistical tests, such as $t$ tests, indicate that the probability is high that any differences between the two groups on each victim variable are due to chance fluctuations, then listwise deletion can be used because victim age is not significantly different for cleared and uncleared cases.

In other words, it is reasonably certain that the missing values in the data set of 65 cases are not having a biasing effect. Among statisticians who have developed models for missing data, this condition is known as Missing Completely at Random (MCAR) (Little & Rubin, 1987, 1989; Little & Schenker, 1995; Rubin, 1976). Statistical techniques that assume a complete data set can be used, although there is some loss of precision due to the smaller number of cases.

The bad news is that the preceding example represented an unrealistic outcome. While the research is limited, it appears that homicides not cleared by arrest are different from those in which an arrest has been effected. Research by Riedel and Rinehart (1996) and Regoeczi, Silverman, and Kennedy (1996) shows that killings involving another felony such as robbery are less likely to be cleared than homicides without concomitant felonies. The smaller number of arrest clearances occurs because robbery murders frequently occur in times and places with stranger offenders. Therefore, the police have no witnesses or "leads" to follow in subsequent investigations.

Listwise deletion in the preceding example would introduce a substantial bias because it would eliminate most victims of robbery murders from the analysis. This condition, where the missingness of one variable is dependent on the values of another variable, is called Missing at Random or MAR by Little and Rubin (1987).

The MAR condition can be turned to advantage. If missing values of one variable are dependent on the values of another variable, can the better reported variable be used to estimate the missing values on the other variable? The belief that correlated variables can be used to impute or estimate missing values is central to a large number of approaches for estimating missing values (Cohen & Cohen, 1983; Raymond, 1986; Raymond & Roberts, 1987).

For example, Williams and Flewelling (1987) noted that variables denoting whether homicides involved concomitant felonies were better reported than variables denoting prior relationships between victims and offenders. Because robberies and robbery murders frequently involve strangers, they used the felony circumstances in an adjustment formula that took account of the under-reporting of stranger homicides. Recently, Williams and Pampel (1998) have explored alternative measures of compensating for missing data.

## Final Thoughts on Missing Data

Crime researchers have generally not made use of estimation or adjustment techniques to account for missing values. They have, however, structured many of their inquiries to avoid the more serious problems of bias in official records and statistics. One approach is to study victims of crime, rather than offenders, because victim data are less plagued by missing values, at least within the context of reported crime. In other words, there is far more research on crime victims than offenders.

A second approach is to study crimes in which it is likely that information will be available on both victims and offenders. For example, lethal and non-lethal violence involving family members more often results in the arrest of offenders than similar violence between acquaintances and strangers. Hence, more is known about offenders involved in domestic violence than is known about violent attacks by strangers.

This is not to suggest that the research is unimportant. Victim-based inquiries and research on domestic violence represent tests of prominent theories like routine activities (Clarke & Felson, 1993; Felson, 1998; Felson & Cohen, 1980) and a host of efforts to explain violence in intimate relationships (Cardarelli, 1997).

It does suggest, however, that crime researchers have failed to come to terms with the problems of missing data. Because low arrest clearances appear to be a permanent feature of violent crimes, missing values will continue to be a prominent characteristic of offender-related variables. An unwillingness to explore the applicability of the variety of missing data estimation models has the effect of slanting research away from a key player in the crime drama.

Finally, the intricacies of estimating missing values are not without limitations. Estimation approaches rest on the belief that correlations between more completely reported and less completely reported variables form a basis for estimations. But as was noted in discussing pairwise deletion, the correlations represent a subset of the population. Put another way, estimation approaches fundamentally assume that relationships between known values are also true for relationships with unknown values. To what extent that assumption is useful for official records and statistics on crime remains unexplored.

## Longitudinal Research, Linkages and Lost Offenders

Introductory texts in criminal justice and criminology point out that criminal justice procedures from arrest to final disposition are an orderly process that begins with a reported crime, arrest of an offender, detention, trial, and sentence, and ends with the application of sanctions (Adler, Mueller, & Laufer, 1991; Gottfredson, 1999; Senna & Siegel, 1996).

Information collected by organizations at each stage is limited by what the responsible persons believe is relevant to the mission or goals of the organization. Police records reflect responses to complaints and crimes, investigations, and arrests. Likewise, detention centers, courts, probation offices, and prisons have information pursuant to their organizational and legal responsibilities.

The preceding practice of organization-specific information collection poses problems for some types of longitudinal designs. Longitudinal studies are designed to permit observations over time. There are three major types of longitudinal designs. Trend studies are those that study change over time such as annual changes in crime rates over a decade. Cohort studies examine changes in specific populations over time, such as the development of criminal careers of a cohort born in 1950. Finally, panel studies interview the same people repeatedly over a period of time. The best example of a panel design is the National Crime Victimization Survey (Baker, 1999; Champion, 1993; Frankfort-Nachmias & Nachmias, 1996; Hagan, 1997; Maxfield & Babbie, 1998).

What poses the greatest problem is the absence of an integrated record system. For people interested in cohort studies, for example, it is not possible to take a single individual and use a single identifier to track him or her through the entire criminal justice process. There is also no assurance that the person's record will be found in other forms in the same system. Finally, if the person leaves the system and reappears subsequently there is no assurance there will be a record of his or her prior involvement. The following sections explore the problem of linkages within the same reporting system and linkages between reporting systems.

## Intra-System Linkages

The Uniform Crime Reporting (UCR) program requests information from police departments using three major forms, as noted in Chapter 3: Return A: Crimes Known to the Police, and Age, Sex, Race, and Ethnic Origin of Arrested Offenders. Unlike these first two, which provide aggregated monthly numbers on all serious crimes, the third form, Supplementary Homicide Reports (SHR), provides detailed information on each homicide case, such as age, race/ethnicity of each victim and offender, circumstances, victim/offender relationships, and weapon used (Riedel, 1999).

There is no provision in any of these forms for linking cases together. Thus, those persons arrested and reported on the Age, Race, Sex, and Ethnic Origin of Persons Arrested cannot be linked to crimes reported on Return A or, in the case of homicides, to information reported on the SHR.

There is no linkage *within* some forms. Hence, the number of crimes reported on Return A as cleared in a month are not linked to the number of crimes reported in the same month. This gives rise to the anomalous finding when examining some months that there are more homicides cleared by arrest than reported.

Comparisons of SHRs to police homicide records for specific cities indicate a high level of agreement between the two sources for total homicides reported: Ratios of SHR frequencies to police record frequencies ranged from 0.97 to 1.07. Comparisons in seven cities between the two data sources indicated highest agreement for gender and lowest for age and weapon totals (Zahn & Riedel, 1983).

The most consistent result is an under-reporting of stranger homicides on the SHR in comparison to police records. This may reflect a reporting lag in that it takes more time to arrest an offender and obtain information on prior victim-offender relationships than other types of homicide. In the absence of a systematic updating program, police files are corrected but the information is not forwarded to the UCR program (Riedel, 1993).

## Inter-System Linkages

Unlike other crime information, homicide information in the United States is collected locally and nationally using two systems. The first is the UCR, which has been described, and the second is mortality statistics. Mortality statistics are gathered by coroners or medical examiners and recorded on death certificates. The national data are published as *Vital Statistics of the United States* by the National Center for Health Statistics (NCHS; Riedel, 1999).

There is no common identifier for the two data sources. It is possible to determine the extent to which both sources report the same phenomena by examining aggregated data. Thus comparisons of annual frequencies since 1976 indicate that NCHS reports about 4% more homicides than Return A and 13% more homicides than the SHR. Dividing Return A estimates by SHR annual counts resulted in a mean ratio of 1.08 or 8% more cases reported by Return A than by the SHR. In other words, there is more agreement between inter-system reporting forms: NCHS totals versus Return A (4%), than between intra-system reporting forms in the UCR: Return A versus SHR (8%) (Riedel, 1999).

### Geographical Variations: Rap Sheet Data

As offenders move in and out of the criminal justice process at different times and places, they accrue criminal histories or rap sheets. But there are substantial problems with this data source. Rap sheets are sometimes missing, there are conflicts between sets of rap sheets kept locally and statewide, and there is the frequent absence of final disposition or incarceration data.

In one of the few studies of its type, Geerken (1994) details additional difficulties. In establishing a criminal history database for a study of New Orleans offenders, Geerken brought together criminal history information from local, state, and FBI systems. Through painstaking matching on a number of individual identifiers, he was able to assemble a population of all offenders arrested at least once for burglary or armed robbery in New Orleans during the 14-year period from 1973 through 1986. Because of the predominantly decentralized state-based approach to maintaining criminal history records that exists in the United States, he was able to show the shortcomings associated with relying on local systems.

A record of arrests is influenced by the geographic mobility of offenders. If offenders are geographically mobile, arrests in one jurisdiction may not be found in the records of another jurisdiction. The potential distortion is evidenced by Geerken's finding that 16.9% of arrests for burglary and armed robbery in 1985 in New Orleans involved offenders born in another state. He found large age and racial variations: whites and older offenders committing crimes in New Orleans were much more likely to have moved there from out-of-state locations.

The author drew two samples and calculated rates for burglary and armed robbery. For a 1985 sample, he calculated the number of *prior arrests* using rap sheet data. For a 1974 sample, he calculated rates for the same offenses for the *subsequent 5 years.*

Geerken then compared rates using New Orleans rap sheet data with all arrests in the more comprehensive data set. For both the prior arrest rates and the rearrest rates, the ratios of black arrests to white arrests were almost doubled when local data were used. However, when all arrests were used, the ratio was substantially lowered and for the prior arrests measure, almost eliminated.

Comparisons were also made by age groups, and there was a tendency for the age-crime relationship to be exaggerated for the post-arrest sample and under-estimated for the prior arrest group. Given the geographical mobility and the inability or unwillingness of criminal history information systems to cope with the problem, local rap sheets pose severe limitations for research, and statewide rap sheets need to be used with sensitivity to the geographic mobility issue.

### False Positive and False Negative Errors

There is a substantial number of *legal* remedies for false positives, that is, people who have been arrested for an offense they did not commit. However, the existence of false positives is not necessarily reflected in official records. As part of the National Youth Survey, Elliott's (1995) research team showed all respondents their rap sheets and asked them to confirm each arrest. They found that 27% of arrests were challenged. In most instances, the respondents acknowledged the legal event, but claimed it was unfounded, a mistake, or they had been told the charges were dropped and they never went to court. Elliott relates the following:

> a young man told us that he had purchased a motorcycle from a private party and had an accident on his way home. He was unconscious at the scene and was taken to the local hospital. The next day two police officers came to arrest him for vehicular theft, as they could find no evidence that he owned the motorcycle. They then called the original owner and verified his story. He never heard anything more about it until we showed him his rap sheet with an arrest for vehicular theft. When we checked again with the relevant police agency, we were told that his story might well be true as they almost never clean records from their files or correct them to reflect such an outcome and at this point in time they had no way of verifying what happened. (pp. 5-6)

In most police jurisdictions, there is no attempt to correct errors in the arrest records or to record changes in charges to reflect a change in the disposition of an arrest.

Unlike false positives, false negatives are a failure to record all arrests, and, Geerken (1994) notes, there are no legal consequences for false negative errors. From a research perspective, the failure to record all arrests leads to serious under-estimates of the number of contacts with the criminal justice system.

False negative errors on rap sheets occur by the misidentification of offenders. Where an offender lies about his name, the deception can be discovered by comparison with local fingerprint files. For example, for New Orleans, Geerken found that about 1% of 111,879 offenders lied about their names and were subsequently discovered. Of course, the discovery of the deception depended upon the offender being previously arrested in New Orleans.

For highly mobile offenders, successful deception is more likely. Many jurisdictions rely on state and federal repositories to confirm identities, but this confirmation may be received long after the offender is released. Changes are required in record systems that are not under the control of the booking agency.

A basic problem is that booking agencies have no way of confirming an offender's "real name." Since they do not routinely check birth records, the "real name" is simply the name under which the offender was first arrested. In constructing the data set for the New Orleans study, Geerken found that 26.8% of New Orleans offenders had known aliases. The fact that the number of aliases is positively related to offender age suggests that the criminal careers of older offenders may be substantially under-estimated.

Another problem that leads to false negative errors is the failure of local agencies to submit fingerprint cards or to submit usable ones. Citing other studies, Geerken estimates that 18% of arrests are not reported to central repositories and an additional 11% are rejected as unusable records. He concludes that because of inadequate record keeping, 29% of arrests are not recorded.

## What Can Be Done?

For crime researchers interested in following offenders and victims through the criminal justice process, data obstacles are formidable. If the researcher wants to compile data at the level of cases, there seem to be few other alternatives than collecting sufficient identifying information at, for example, the level of reported crime or arrest. Identifying information, it should be pointed out, should include such variables as name, age, race/ethnicity, and date of arrest.

The task that faces the researcher is similar to that faced by Geerken (1994) in his rap sheet research. It is a difficult, time-consuming, and expensive task to gather data from one agency, then go to other agencies, match cases, and collect data. While the data collection task is difficult in itself, the various steps described in Chapter 4 in accessing official records in each agency have to be considered.

It is possible to avoid some of the problems that plague case tracking research by using a time-series design. In time-series designs, observations of one or more variables are made over time. Thus, trends in indictments for various types of violent crimes can be compared to arrests for these crimes to examine prosecutorial performance. The strengths and limitations of various types of longitudinal designs are discussed in the research methods books cited previously.

There is, in addition, reason to believe that UCR data will be better in the future. As was noted in Chapter 3, the National Incident-Based Reporting System (NIBRS), which will eventually replace the current UCR program, links together all segments of the incident with originating agency identifiers, incident numbers, and sequence numbers where multiple victims and offenders are involved. While a linking identifier in NIBRS will eliminate many of the problems in the current UCR program, I know of nothing to address the problem of having two systems (UCR and NCHS) report the same event, homicide, yet have nothing that permits users to identify the case in the two systems.

The problems outlined by Geerken in his study of rap sheets are formidable. Perhaps Geerken gives the most useful advice in suggesting the use of statewide criminal history information rather than local data, although that does not alleviate the problem of offenses and offenders getting lost because of geographical mobility.

# 6

# LEGAL DIMENSIONS OF SECONDARY DATA

The access, use, and analysis of secondary data raise a number of potential legal issues. This chapter discusses two legal issues that typically do not receive a great deal of attention in traditional methods courses: freedom of information acts and subpoenas. Freedom of information acts provide tremendous opportunities for researchers interested in accessing government records. Yet, along with subpoenas, freedom of information acts also represent potential legal threats that data will be made public against a researcher's will. Freedom of information acts and threats are discussed in that order.

## Freedom of Information Acts

The federal and state freedom of information acts (FOIAs) can be friends to researchers interested in secondary data. As noted, a great deal of public data are available to researchers interested in secondary data analysis. Yet, there may arise the need to resort to legal means when data desired from agencies are not made accessible. For researchers, the potential uses of federal and state freedom of information acts are limited only by the imagination and the information available. During the debate over the 1974 Amendments, Senator Kennedy noted,

> The processes of Government touch almost every aspect of our lives, every day. From the food we eat to the cars we drive to the air we breathe; Federal agencies constantly monitor and regulate and control. . . . And it generates tons of paperwork as it goes about its business. The Freedom of Information Act guarantees citizen access to Government information and provides the key for unlocking the doors to a vast storeroom of information.[1]

Some examples of the way the federal FOIA has been used in the past include using the FOIA (a) to ensure agency performance of statutory responsibilities and to expose possible government wrong-doing, (b) to obtain agency records of use by investigative reporters, (c) to obtain records for use in historical work, (d) to obtain records for use in academic studies, (e) to obtain records for use by public interest groups, (f) to obtain information from an agency at a lower cost than if obtained from other sources, and (g) to obtain names of persons for litigation purposes (Adler, 1995). Similar uses have been made of state freedom of information acts.

## Federal Freedom of Information Act

When the federal Freedom of Information Act went into effect in 1967, a statutory right of access by *any* person to federal agency records was established. As noted by one court, "Congress granted the scholar and the scoundrel equal rights of access to agency records" (*Dunns v. Bureau of Prisons*, 1986). The basic concept behind the enactment of the FOIA was that *all* records of agencies of the federal government would be accessible to the public unless specifically exempt from this requirement. Moreover, the person requesting the information generally need not even state a reason for the request. As long as some public interest can be discerned, the request is proper. Requests for purely commercial purposes (e.g., a request to compile names for a mailing list) may be denied.

The federal FOIA specifies that researchers reasonably describe the records sought and that requests be made in accordance with agencies' published procedural regulations. Each federal agency must publish its procedural regulations for gaining access to records under the FOIA. The regulation must inform the public of where and how to address requests as well as what records are maintained. In addition, federal agencies must publish the schedule of fees to be charged for a search, review, and duplication. They also must publish any fee waiver criteria and the administrative appeal process for denied requests. In disclosing information, agencies employ one of three options: (a) publishing in the *Federal Register;* (b) making information available for public inspection and copying; or (c) releasing information pursuant to a request from any person.

However, it is important to note that not all data are subject to disclosure. The mere process of gathering data pursuant to federal funding does not necessarily qualify the data as an agency record subject to disclosure under the federal FOIA.[2] The data must first be transferred to a government agency before a record is officially created. The U.S. Supreme Court has developed a two-part test for determining what constitutes an "agency record": Agency records are records either created or obtained by an agency, and under agency control at the time of the request (*U.S. Dept. of Justice v. Tax Analysts*, 1989).

Moreover, the mere physical location of material alone is insufficient to transform data into "agency records." In *Forsham v. Harris* (1980), the Supreme Court held that data generated by a privately controlled organization that had received federal grants, but which data had not at any time been obtained by the agency, were not "agency records" accessible under the FOIA. The Court acknowledged that even though the agency could have at any time obtained the data and created agency records, it did not do so and was therefore not compelled to disclose the data. Thus, the determining question is whether the agency relies on or uses the data. "An agency must either create or obtain a record as a prerequisite to it becoming an 'agency record' within the meaning of the FOIA" (*Forsham v. Harris*, 1980, p. 183).

The Court also looked to the definition of "agency record" contained in the Record Disposal Act, 44 U.S.C. Sec. 3301 et seq. to determine Congressional intent. The Act defines an agency record as materials made or received by an agency that should be preserved (or are appropriate for preservation) by the agency "as evidence of the organization, functions, policies, decisions, procedures, operations, or other activities of the Government or because of the informational value of data in them."

In one case, a group of non-profit, church-related organizations sought empirical information about differences in breast-fed and formula-fed infants. The information was to help determine whether the feeding pattern could be correlated with morbidity and mortality and to find out whether particular marketing practices influence the choice of a particular feeding pattern. There was no governmental participation in the drafting or the eventual design of the survey; the project was not government funded; nor was there any governmental participation in the collection of data, the interviewing of 1,650 low-income mothers.

The principal investigator charged with the analysis of the data contacted the Centers for Disease Control (CDC) in Atlanta to perform the conversion of data to computer tape and perform the appropriate statistical analysis. In exchange for the analysis, the CDC was to retain a copy of the tape. Later, the CDC and the principal investigator agreed that the CDC would only convert the data to tape and forgo any analysis.

When the project neared completion, Mead Johnson & Co. and Abbott Laboratories, two infant formula producers, requested copies of the tape under the federal Freedom of Information Act. The understanding of the principal investigator was that the companies would receive the report only after the analysis was completed and published. The CDC felt that they had to comply with the FOIA request. The judge who ultimately decided the issue found that the FOIA required disclosure to the companies. Thus, what began as a privately sponsored research project ended with compelled discovery of information (*St. Paul's Benevolent Educational and Missionary Institute v. United States,* 1980). The data were considered to be an agency record because the CDC did create the record (tape) and was intending to utilize the information.

Although any person for just about any reason can obtain information contained in a government agency record, the FOIA specifically lists nine exemptions under which an agency may withhold information from an FOIA requester. 5 U.S.C. Sec. 552 (C)(b)(1)-(b)(9) lists the following exemptions:

1. (a) specifically authorized under criteria established by an Executive order to be kept secret in the interest of national defense or foreign policy and (b) are in fact properly classified pursuant to such Executive order;
2. "related solely to the internal personnel rules and practices of an agency";
3. "specifically exempted from disclosure by statute" other than the FOIA, provided that such statute (a) required that the matters be withheld from the public in such a manner as to leave no discretion on the issue, or (b) established particular criteria for withholding or refers to particular types of matters to be withheld;
4. "trade secrets and commercial or financial information obtained from a person and privileged or confidential"[3];
5. "inter-agency or intra-agency memorandums or letters" that would be privileged in civil litigation;
6. "personnel and medical and similar files the disclosure of which would constitute a clearly unwarranted invasion of personal privacy";

7. "records or information compiled for law enforcement purposes," but only to the extent that one or more of six specified
   forms of harm would result from disclosure;
8. "contained in or related to examination, operating, or condition
   reports prepared by, on behalf of, or for the use of an agency
   responsible for the regulation or supervision of financial institutions"; or
9. "geological and geophysical information and data, including
   maps, concerning wells."

Of the nine exemptions, two are especially applicable to social science researchers interested in criminal justice secondary data analysis, Exemption 6 and Exemption 7.

### Exemption 6

As noted, Exemption 6 exempts "personnel and medical and similar files the disclosure of which would constitute a clearly unwarranted invasion of personal privacy." Most of the early cases
interpreting Exemption 6 do not directly involve criminal justice
research data, but the issues that emerge provide a useful guide to the
process courts apply when considering requests.

In *Dept. of State v. Washington Post,* the U.S. Supreme Court was
asked to decide whether passports of Iranian nationals satisfied the
"similar files" requirement contained in Exemption 6. The Court held
that passports were "similar files" for the purpose of the FOIA. In so
holding, the Court gave a broad construction to the requirement that
information need be contained in a "personnel," "medical," or "similar" file.[4] Indeed, the construction is so broad that, functionally, subsequent courts interpreting the FOIA are all but ignoring the
classification of the type of file and instead are focusing on the
records contained in the file.

In the aftermath of the Court's holding in *Washington Post,* courts
are holding that any information about a *particular individual* contained in an agency file may be considered to constitute a clearly

unwarranted invasion of personal privacy (Adler, 1995). Thus, once
an FOIA request is found to yield information about a particular individual, the courts undertake the next step to determine whether the
information falls under Exemption 6.[5]

The next step involves considering whether disclosing information about a particular individual constitutes an unwarranted invasion of personal privacy. For this determination, courts employ a
balancing test. The test balances the competing interests of individual privacy against the public's right to know. In conducting the balancing test, cases are uniform in giving strict construction to the
language in the exemption requiring that the privacy invasion be
"clearly unwarranted." The majority of cases have held that this language—"clearly unwarranted"—instructs the court to tilt the balance in favor of disclosure (Adler, 1995).

Given such a liberal test, attempts to protect promises and expectations for confidentiality have not fared well in general, though they
have not been extensively tested.[6] Specific promises of confidentiality made to respondents in the course of research have yet to be litigated, though a court's treatment would probably not differ from
other cases in which promises of confidentiality were given. In one
case, the Department of Health and Human Services promised confidentiality to grant reviewers who completed a "Confidential Statement of Employment and Financial Interests." The statement was
necessary in order to discover possible conflicts of interests. In balancing all of the interests, the court considered the pledge of confidentiality as affecting only a minor interest:

> To be sure, the consultants' expectations of privacy were heightened
> by the government's pledge of confidentiality. Other things being
> equal, release of information provided under a pledge of confidential-
> ity involves a greater invasion of privacy than release of information
> provided without such a pledge. On the other hand, to allow the gov-
> ernment to make documents exempt by the simple method of promis-
> ing confidentiality would subvert FOIA's disclosure mandate. On
> balance, we believe that a government pledge of confidentiality, made

in good faith and consistently honored, should generally be given weight on the privacy side of the scale in accord with its effect on expectations of privacy. (*Washington Post Co. v. Dept. of HHS*, 1982)

The expectation of confidence in this case was somewhat limited. The reviewers were told that the information would be held confidential absent "good cause." The question remains open as to how much weight will be given higher expectations of confidentiality.

In another case, an FOIA requester demanded access to the identities of rejected grant applicants to test the hypothesis that unorthodox proposals were generally refused. The names were eventually revealed, as the court believed the rejected grant applicants to have very little privacy interests in the disclosure of their identities. Exemption 6 was interpreted to apply to only information that contained "intimate details" of a "highly personal" nature (*Kurzon v. Dept. of Health and Human Serv.*, 1981).

Even when courts acknowledge that some privacy interest bears protection, the analysis does not end with such a finding. When unwarranted invasions of personal privacy are found, the offending portion may be segregated, and the information still released. Immediately following the enumeration of FOIA exemptions, Sec. 552(b) provides that "Any reasonably segregable portion of a record shall be provided to any person requesting such record after deletion of the portions which are exempt under this subsection."

Almost all courts have held the personal privacy interests protected by Exemption 6 and the similar clause found in Exemption 7(C) lapse upon the death of the individual. However, in a few cases, courts have upheld claims of Exemption 6 based on privacy interests of surviving family members. For example, NASA successfully fought off requests to release tape recordings of voices of astronauts of the final flight of the Space Shuttle *Challenger* (*New York Times v. NASA*, 1991). The court noted that transcripts had already been released and the sounds on the tape were irrelevant to the conduct of any government agency or official being investigated.

### Exemption 7

Amendments were made to Exemption 7 as part of the Anti-Drug Abuse Act of 1986 to strengthen protection of data and to refer directly to law enforcement records. Exemption 7 provides that the FOIA does not apply to

> records or information compiled for law enforcement purposes, but only to the extent that the production of such law enforcement records or information (A) could reasonably be expected to interfere with enforcement proceedings, (B) would deprive a person of a right to a fair trial or an impartial adjudication, (C) could reasonably be expected to constitute an unwarranted invasion of personal privacy, (D) could reasonably be expected to disclose the identity of a confidential source, including a state, local, or foreign agency or authority or any private institution which furnished information on a confidential basis, and, in the case of a record or information compiled by a criminal law enforcement authority in the course of a criminal investigation or by an agency conducting a lawful national security intelligence investigation, information furnished by a confidential source, (E) would disclose techniques and procedures for law enforcement investigations or prosecutions, or would disclose guidelines for law enforcement investigations or prosecutions if such disclosure could reasonably be expected to risk circumvention of the law, or (F) could reasonably be expected to endanger the life or physical safety of any individual.

With these six standards, Exemption 7 places fairly severe restrictions on the secondary data researcher interested in accessing records related to law enforcement. Moreover, courts have interpreted Exemption 7 in ways that further reduce disclosure. For example, although the Freedom of Information Act might be construed to apply only to records held by the federal government, at least one court has interpreted Exemption 7 to apply to all law enforcement records—federal, state, or local—that lie within the possession of the federal government (*Wojtczak v. Dept. of Justice*, 1982).

In determining the applicability of Exemption 7, the initial inquiry is whether the requested records or information is compiled for law enforcement purposes. Although what constitutes "information" is subject to disagreement, as noted, the purpose of the amendments was to provide greater protection of data. Thus, even law enforcement techniques and procedures (including manuals) are likely now to be protected from disclosure.

The question arises as to what happens to information that is initially compiled for non-law enforcement purposes and later becomes used for investigation. For example, a routine contractor audit subsequently became part of an investigatory file compiled for a law enforcement purpose. In 1989, the Supreme Court rejected the distinction

> between documents that originally were assembled for law enforcement purposes and those that were not so originally assembled but were gathered later for such purposes. The plain language of Exemption 7 does not permit such a distinction. Under the statute, documents need only to have been compiled when the response to the FOIA request must be made. (*John Doe Agency v. John Doe Corp*, 1989, p. 155)

In dissent, Justice Scalia noted that agencies need only gather up documents they do not wish to disclose with a plausible law enforcement purpose in mind to evade disclosure successfully. The extent to which this happens is unknown, but it is clear that the consequence is less access for secondary data researchers.

Even if FOIA requests fall within the definition of records or information compiled for law enforcement purposes, the materials may not be exempt from disclosure unless they cause some harm embodied in one of Exemption 7's six standards regarding protected law enforcement interests. Given the comprehensive nature of these six standards, this does not appear to be a difficult task.

For example, a significant Supreme Court case deals with interpreting Exemption 7's provision that records or information may be withheld if disclosure could "(C) reasonably be expected to constitute an unwarranted invasion of personal privacy." At issue was a request for an individual rap sheet maintained by the FBI. The Court held

> as a categorical matter that a third party's request for law enforcement records or information about a private citizen can reasonably be expected to invade that citizen's privacy, and that when the request seeks no "official information" about a government agency, but merely records that the government happens to be storing, the invasion of privacy is unwarranted. (*Dept. of Justice v. Reporters Committee for Freedom of the Press,* 1989, p. 780)

## State Freedom of Information Acts

Fortunately for researchers, the federal FOIA is not the only game in town. There are also state statutes that contain provisions similar to those found in the federal FOIA. Although the case law interpreting these statutes is not as extensive as that developed for the federal FOIA, a trend of increasing FOIA litigation foreshadows equality in the near future. Every state has some version of the federal freedom of information act (Franklin & Bouchard, 1995). There are similarities as well as differences among the statutes. Almost all are in some way modeled after the federal statute and contain an exemption for "clearly unwarranted invasion of privacy."

The number and specificity of additional exemptions varies considerably between statutes. The Illinois statute, for example, lists 38 different exemptions. Of possible interest to the college or university researcher, listed exemptions include "course materials or research materials used by faculty members," and "valuable formulae, designs, drawings and research data obtained or produced by any public body when disclosure could reasonably be expected to produce private gain or public loss." The exact manner in which these provisions would play out in court can only be speculated upon as the case law on almost all the state acts is sparse.

One commentator, lamenting the paucity of case law on his state's FOIA, partly blames the Commonwealth of Kentucky's Attorney

General. The Attorney General is required to issue an opinion at the request of persons denied access to records. The result has been to confuse further the standard to be applied when balancing the "clearly unwarranted invasion of personal privacy" provision (Comment, 1982-1983).

New York has perhaps the most case law, albeit none dealing directly with social science researchers. The following example, however, illustrates the approach most state courts take in interpreting their statutes as well as a typical use made of most state FOIAs.

In New York, subsequent to a promotional examination for the rank of sergeant, two minority associations instituted a Civil Rights action against the city, alleging discrimination. A court approved settlement of this litigation provided that the police officers on the eligible list would be promoted to sergeant, and that in addition, black and Hispanic officers who had not passed the examination would be placed on Supplementary Eligibility Lists and promoted to sergeant. A police officer requested disclosure of the examination grades of all persons on the supplementary lists. The names of the persons on the lists had already been disclosed. The state agency (Department of Personnel of the City of N.Y.) denied the request on the grounds that such disclosure "would constitute an unwarranted invasion of personal privacy" (*Rainey v. Levitt*, 1988).

Consistent with the liberal philosophy of the federal courts' interpreting federal FOIAs, the state court granted the petition for the disclosure. The court noted that a narrow interpretation of the "unwarranted invasion of personal privacy" provision and a liberal construction of the Freedom of Information Law "compelled" such a conclusion.

### Summary

To summarize, in considering questions of confidentiality of data, courts have focused their inquiry on the interests of the requester and the agency. In research cases, the agency often acts as the guardian of the privacy interest of the respondent. In a typical balancing test, the court will focus on the interest of the requester and the public's right to information and whether the disclosure results in a "clearly unwarranted invasion of personal privacy." The burden is always on the agency to show that the information should be withheld under one of the exemptions. Although promises of confidentiality have not been fully litigated, they are clearly not determinative. Concerning law enforcement records specifically, recent amendments and court decisions indicate that data may be difficult to obtain, but the enormous amount of data collected by federal and state governments should not be overlooked.

## The Threat of Freedom of Information Acts

Just as researchers should be aware of possible uses of FOIAs, they also should remember that FOIAs are double-edged swords: Any research that is generated may become subject to FOIAs. The general harms and costs associated whenever professional breaches of confidentiality occur are considerable. Disclosure of personal information without a respondent's consent has costs to the respondent, the profession, and society. When a researcher fails to inform the respondent that the information provided may not be kept confidential, the individual's right to participate voluntarily has been violated.

In addition, the basic interpersonal relationship between researcher and respondent is abused. This abuse not only diminishes the profession's status as teachers and scientists, but ultimately leads to a loss of trust in the profession. Although the element of intent is absent when breaches of confidentiality are mandated by legal forces not foreseen by the researcher, respondents may still impose a constructive knowledge on the researcher. For them, the harm still occurs. Thus, the researcher either knew or should have known that disclosure was possible.

Moreover, there are harms specific to the context of freedom of information laws. For researchers, disclosure of research data may bring to light information or methods that they did not yet wish to share with either the public or others in the profession. For example, the information may reflect preliminary, politically sensitive data that should not be made public without further study and/or replication. Moreover, premature disclosure of novel methodologies may give impressions of false optimism for those seeking solutions to similar problems. One need only wait for the next spate of AIDS or cancer prevention/cure studies to watch public expectations rise, usually based upon little data.

Released information that is incorrectly analyzed or misinterpreted harms initially the public and ultimately the profession charged with the responsibility of ensuring accuracy. When widespread publication occurs, the problem is compounded. The potential for harm is further increased when unknown flaws or limitations in the methodology are not obvious from the released information. Thus, those relying upon conclusions either inferred from raw data or tentatively stated are at great risk for being misinformed.

For respondents from whom the data were gathered, the chance remains that their privacy will be violated. The extent of the harm depends on the degree of disclosure. The primary threat from freedom of information acts arises when released information reveals information that could identify respondents promised anonymity.[7] Even though names may be withheld, it still may be possible to discern identities through "deductive disclosure." Although names may be withheld, the identities may still be deduced from other demographic variables. The risk for such disclosure is particularly true in longitudinal and outcome studies.

The disclosure of such information may not only harm the present respondents but also may inhibit future data collection because of concerns over confidentiality. Even if confidentiality is not an issue, the release of information may affect future responses. By making public the responses of previous subjects, future respondents may alter their responses.

An additional danger inheres for those submitting research proposals. As noted, "all" federal records are accessible unless
exempted. Thus, whenever a researcher submits any information to a
federal agency, the information may become part of a government
record. As a government record, the information is obtainable under
the FOIA and may therefore be disclosed to a requesting party. For
example, a research proposal for government grant support has been
held to be an "agency record" for the purpose of the FOIA.[8]

As warned by some authors,

> the researcher who submits a grant or contract proposal to the federal
> government must realize that although the evaluations of grant
> reviewers and site visitors need not be disclosed, the research rationale
> and hypotheses, the design, operationalizations of independent and
> dependent variables, sampling techniques, and any scales that may
> have been developed in pilot work—in short, all parts of the pro-
> posal—are available to anyone upon request. This makes for several
> interesting possibilities. One is an unscrupulous colleague stealing a
> researcher's "breakthrough" theories or methods. Another is a
> researcher's local press finding out about his or her controversial
> hypotheses and plans for research and then either misinforming the
> public about them [cite omitted] or poisoning the subject pool by mak-
> ing subjects aware of the hypotheses of the study. (Morris, Sales, & Ber-
> man, 1981, p. 822)

## The Threat of Subpoenas

A second potential legal threat involves the use of subpoenas, judicial orders that command researchers to provide data to courts when
such information is relevant to central issues in litigation. No academic discipline is immune from compelled disclosure of research
data by subpoena. As with confidentiality, the potential dangers with
subpoenas arise primarily when researchers access survey data and
official records.

To resolve legal disputes, courts are granted wide latitude under
civil and criminal rules of procedure to gather evidence relevant to
issues in controversy. However, there are some protections against

compelled disclosure. First, research data may be protected if the data are subject to privilege, as specified by federal or state statutes. For example, the Public Heath Service Act provides as follows:

> The Secretary [of Health and Human Services] may authorize persons engaged in biomedical, behavioral, clinical, or other research (including research on the use and effect of alcohol and other psychoactive drugs) to protect the privacy of individuals who are the subject of such research by withholding from all persons not connected with the conduct of such research, the names, or other identifying characteristics of such individuals. Persons so authorized to protect the privacy of such individuals may not be compelled in any federal, state or local civil, criminal, administrative, legislative, or other proceeding to identify such individuals.

In order to preserve the confidentiality of research subjects, researchers must request a certificate of confidentiality from the Department of Health and Human Services.

A second protection lies within the purview of the court. Courts must make a determination as to whether the burden of compelling the disclosure of the data is outweighed by the need for the information. This determination primarily rests on balancing the inconvenience of requiring the researcher to provide the data against the probative value of the information to a specific issue in need of resolution.

A primary concern regarding such disclosure is that researchers may be forced to violate the confidentiality promised to participating subjects regarding the use of the data collected. In one case, a researcher argued unsuccessfully that the disclosure would result in a breach of the promise of confidentiality, the disruption of the data collection, and the destruction of the data set for future studies. An appellate court disagreed and ordered the lower court to fashion an order that would turn over non-identifiable research data to permit a review of the research methodology (*Deitchman v. Squibb & Sons*, 1984).

Cases in which courts compel disclosure of social science secondary data are uncommon. Most research, particularly in the criminal justice arena, is rarely directly relevant to issues in criminal and civil litigation. Indeed, one of the advantages of secondary analysis is that it allows independent assessment of the original research findings and thus provides courts a reason not to compel the production of original data.

## Conclusions

Although researchers are often in the position of requesting information through freedom of information acts, researchers should also be aware of measures they may take to protect data from disclosure from either FOIA requests or subpoenas. The following steps are offered to minimize the risk of data being unduly disclosed.

The first task is to identify all the places where the data may eventually land and what threats exist. Thus, if a federal or state agency is involved, it may become necessary to familiarize oneself with the applicable freedom of information acts and appropriate exemptions. This may prove difficult, but should be done in order that confidentiality not be violated; all of the risks of disclosure should be made known to subjects prior to obtaining informed consent.

Another tactic is to secure promises of confidentiality from any relevant agency. Although they have not yet been held to be highly probative, they present to the court some evidence of the seriousness in which the confidentiality is held. Specifically, if applicable, obtain a certificate of confidentiality from the Department of Health and Human Services, which may be used by researchers to protect the "names or other identifying characteristics of . . . individuals" who participate in mental health research.[9] However, research data per se are not protected, and the impact of these certificates on the balancing process has yet to be litigated.

If possible, minimize the direct contact that the agency has with the data being collected. Remember, even if the data are being collected for an agency, the data must first become a record. A record is only created by an agency's actual use or creation of the record. In addition, attempts should be made to disguise data. If this is not possible, the researcher may be able to demonstrate to a court that "unwarranted invasion of personal privacy" will occur through deductive disclosure.

Another option is to file a "reverse" FOIA suit. A reverse FOIA suit asks a court to balance competing interests before disclosure occurs. A researcher may file a lawsuit when an agency has decided to disclose information that either is not encompassed by the FOIA; or for which the FOIA, though applicable, does not mandate disclosure; or when such disclosure would violate a non-disclosure statute. In many cases a researcher is able to, and for strategic reasons may want to, file a reverse FOIA action before the requester is able to file an FOIA action.

Finally, it is important to stay in touch with any agency that may receive the data. This will allow the researcher to be aware of any developing legal threats of disclosure and to take appropriate measures. Thus, with some foreplanning, threats to disclosure may be minimized, though never eliminated altogether.

## Notes

1. *Freedom of Information Act and Amendments of 1974 (P.L. 93-502) Source Book: Legislative History, Texts, and Other Documents* (Joint Comm. Print 1975) at 284-285.

2. See, for example, *Ciba-Geigy v. Mathews*, 428 F.Supp. 523 (S.D.N.Y. 1977) and *Forsham v. Califano*, 587 F.2d 1128 (D.C. Cir. 1978), 405 U.S. 169 (1980). The plaintiffs in both cases alleged that federal funding gave the University Group Diabetes Program the characteristics of an "agency" whose records would be responsive to the FOIA and that even if the Group was not an agency, the federal funding of, access to, control of, and reliance on the findings made the data equivalent to agency records—this in spite of the clear statement of the grantees' property rights in the grant application. Both district courts held that although the grant document established the right of access in the granting agency to the records of the grantees for audits and other purposes, it was held that prior to the exercise of that right the raw data did not constitute agency records.

3. A discussion of the relevance of Exemption 4 can be found in Cecil and Griffin (1985), "The Role of Legal Policies in Data Sharing": "Thus, it appears that the trade secret exemption to the Freedom of Information Act will not restrict the release of agency research information when that data is not identifiable unless such release might 'impair the government's ability to obtain necessary information in the future' or substantially harm a business's competitive position. In the few instances in which the courts have limited access under these interpretations, there were circumstances that are unlikely to be present when most researchers seek access to agency records" (p. 160).

4. *Dept. of State v. Washington Post,* 456 U.S. 595 (1982): "When disclosure of information which applies to a particular individual is sought from Government records, courts must determine whether release of the information would constitute a clearly unwarranted invasion of that person's privacy" (Id. at 602). The Court concluded that "[t]his construction of Exemption 6 will not render meaningless the threshold requirement that information be contained in personnel, medical, and similar files" because "[i]nformation unrelated to any particular person presumably would not satisfy the threshold test" (Id. at 4).

5. See, for example, *Hemenway v. Hughes,* 601 F.Supp. 1002, 1005, (D.D.C. 1985) ("to survive the initial inquiry the agency need only establish that the records in question apply to a particular individual"). Similarly, the Courts of Appeal are now routinely holding such matters as names and addresses to be "similar files," and then proceeding with a balancing test. *Minnesota v. U.S. Dept. of Agriculture,* 737 F.2d 784, 786 (9th Cir. 1984), *Van Bourg, Allen, Weinberg & Roger v. NLRB,* 728 F.2d 1270, 1272 (9th Cir. 1984), *Berry v. Dept. of Justice,* 733 F.2d 1343, 1353 (9th Cir. 1984) (presentence report is similar file).

6. A prior promise of confidentiality, while sometimes relevant to the degree of invasion of personal privacy, is not determinative and cannot be used to frustrate the policy of the Act. See, for example, *Citizens for Environ. Quality v. U.S. Dept. of Agriculture,* 602 F. Supp. 534, 538 (D.D.C. 1984); *Legal Aid Society of Alameda County v. Schults,* 349 F. Supp. 771, 776 (N.D. Cal. 1972); *Providence Journal Co. v. FBI,* 460 F. Supp 786 (D.R.I. 1978).

"It will obviously not be enough for the agency to assert simply that it received the file under a pledge of confidentiality to the ones who supplied it. Undertakings of that nature cannot, in and of themselves, override the Act" (*Ackerly v. Ley,* 420 F.2d 1336, 1339-40 n.3 [D.C. Cir. 1969]).

Knowledge of the proposed disclosure plus lack of objection may weaken confidentiality (*Robles v. EPA,* 484 F.2d 843, 847 [4th Cir. 1973]), as may partial disclosure (*Simpson v. Vance,* 648 F.2d 10, 16 [D.C. 1980]).

7. The threat of specific names being released is diminished by the powers granted agencies under the Privacy Act. Under the Privacy Act, names may not be released unless they fall under an exemption. No specific exemption exists for research.

8. *Washington Research Project v. Department of Health, Education, and Welfare,* 504 F.2d 238 (D.C. Cir. 1974) cert denied, 421 U.S. 963 (1975) "Research designs submitted in grant applications are not exempt from disclosure under the Act. This holding

extends to all types of applications—initial, continuation, supplemental, and renewal—and to progress reports made by grantees as part of the last three kinds of applications" (Id. at 245). The FOIA request sought information about the grant as well as reports of the site visitation.

9. 42 U.S.C. Sec. 242a (1982). Researchers interested in applying for a certificate of confidentiality should write to: Extramural Policy Branch, National Institute of Mental Health, Rm. 9-95, 5600 Fishers Lane, Rockville, MD 20851.

# THE FUTURE OF
# SECONDARY DATA

A s noted in the first chapter, the use of secondary data is standard fare in history and eco-
nomics. The use of secondary data for crime research seems to have
developed from criminology's historically close relationships to sociology and, specifically, with a concern for secondary analysis of
social surveys. Hyman's (1972) book, *Secondary Analysis of Sample
Surveys,* has been among the most frequently cited books on the topic.

Writing at about the same time, Finifter (1975, p. 119) leaves the
impression that secondary analysis was not a popular approach
among sociologists. Commenting on the fact that the supply of
archived data is exceeding the demand from researchers, he says,

> Several explanations for this paradox have been suggested including
> the stigma attached to "secondary" analysis as if it were a presumed
> inferior second cousin to "primary" analysis; a corresponding per-
> verse infatuation with novelty and originality; textbooks and profes-
> sional socialization programs that ignore or denigrate secondary

analysis; prejudice of research funding toward collecting "fresh" data instead of analyzing existing data, and the reluctance of many researchers to conform their research interests to the possibilities afforded by available data.

It is difficult to account for the beliefs that Finifter describes. Social science researchers are trained in a wide variety of methods of observation and spend much of their time trying to ascertain the validity and reliability of the observations. It may be that the sociology of the time Finifter describes was more concerned about its scientific status and more concerned about the "scientific" character of its observations than is presently true. Yet because observations are made by non-researchers and practitioners, it does not follow that they are invalid and unreliable. Validity and reliability have to be settled by empirical inquiry, not by the social status of observers. Social science researchers, it must be said, are not the only people who can observe accurately and reliably!

Criminology and criminal justice also have a different relationship to secondary data in comparison to sociology. The initial concern with secondary data for sociologists was the analysis of social surveys; for crime researchers, the ongoing concern is with problems of access, data quality, and data collection. Because so much of what crime researchers study is available as information collected for another purpose, the focus shifts from analysis to what is done before analysis can occur.

While it is always risky to predict the future of any social phenomenon, there are changes that suggest increasing secondary data use. Specifically, there has been an increase in the willingness of federal agencies to provide data sets; an increase in the number of qualified users; and a revolution in computing technology that makes secondary data easier to access and use.

## The Contribution of Funding Agencies

During the first 3 months of 1999, there were 7,241 users accessing studies at the Inter-university Consortium for Political and Social

Research (ICPSR). For the same period, there were 548 users accessing 648 studies available at the National Archive of Criminal Justice Data (NACJD) *(http://www.icpsr.umich.edu/NACJD/top.html)*.

While this was discussed in greater detail in Chapter 2, one of the reasons that ICPSR and NACJD have grown to their present size is the contributions of federal criminal justice agencies. ICPSR has made agreements with a wide range of federal agencies to deposit data with the Consortium. With the Bureau of Justice Statistics and the National Institute of Justice leading the way, data from funded research projects are now routinely deposited in the archive. For example, the Data Resources Program of the National Institute of Justice began in 1984 to archive all data sets from funded projects.

## An Increase in the Number of Qualified Users

At the level of the individual researcher, it is likely that disciplines will never again see the level of funding for research on crime that occurred in the late sixties and the seventies through the Law Enforcement Assistance Administration. While lavish spending led to an enormous increase in the number of people working and researching in criminal justice, the decline of research funding left them with fewer opportunities for research. When the latter is combined with continued and frequently higher standards for research to achieve academic tenure and promotion, the use of secondary data became an inexpensive and easily accessible alternative.

While not all crime researchers belong to professional associations with "criminal justice" or "criminology" in the title, the size of the membership is an indication of the number of possible secondary data users. The paid membership of the American Society of Criminology, one of two major professional organizations in criminology and criminal justice, ranged between 2,000 and 3,200 members during the years from 1987 through 1999.[1] However, the greatest increase in the number of qualified users is due to the appearance of another discipline: criminal justice.

## Criminal Justice: Growth and Changes

Prior to 1967, criminal justice and criminology programs were few and primarily associated with sociology departments. The sole source of governmental research funds was the Center for Crime and Delinquency of the National Institute of Mental Health. The major impetus for the growth of criminal justice programs and research occurred in 1967 when the Omnibus Crime Control and Safe Streets Act was signed into law. The Law Enforcement Assistance Administration was the federal agency given the responsibility of carrying out the Act. "Few watersheds in the history of any discipline can be so precisely dated as the transformation of criminal justice studies under the powerful influence of the Law Enforcement Assistance Administration" (Conrad & Myren, 1979, p. 7).

The 1967 legislation made possible funding of a large number of crime-related educational programs. Conrad and Myren (1979) show that the number of associate degree programs rose from 152 in 1966-1967 to 1,209 in 1979-1980, and baccalaureate programs increased from 39 to 589. Conrad and Myren were undoubtedly correct in concluding that "this may well be the most rapid growth ever experienced in any substantive academic area in the history of higher education in the United States" (p. 24).

Early associate degree programs focused on training police and corrections personnel (Bennett & Marshall, 1979; Morn, 1980). By 1979, John Conrad and Richard Myren (1979) were discussing the relationship between criminology and criminal justice and how the latter should abandon an agency orientation and move in the direction of greater curricula content in the social sciences and humanities. Their discussions reflected differing views of criminal justice and criminology rather than a debate on whether graduate programs should exist, the latter having already been established in several universities.

Most of the early doctoral programs were established in the east. The State University of New York at Albany began implementation of its doctoral program in 1966. The City University of New York changed the name of its program to the John Jay College of Criminal Justice in 1966. American University established its Center for the Administration of Justice in 1969, and Michigan State University School of Police Administration and Public Safety became the School of Criminal Justice in 1970.

All these doctoral programs followed a traditional emphasis on developing and practicing research skills. Such an emphasis apparently also reflected the beliefs of people in the field. In a survey of between 535 and 538 members of the Academy of Criminal Justice Sciences by Gordon Misner, respondents were asked to rank their amount of disagreement (0) or agreement (10) to a series of items about criminal justice education. While there was disagreement (3.98) that research should be a program commitment at the community college level, they expressed agreement (6.29) that it should be a program commitment at the 4-year level, and even greater agreement (7.68) at the graduate level (cited in Conrad & Myren, 1979, pp. 32-33).

With the appearance and rapid growth of a discipline, there were inevitable questions about whether, in fact, it was a discipline and its relationship to criminology. Discussions by Morn (1980), Bennett and Marshall (1979), and Conrad and Myren (1979) tried to delineate and distinguish similarities and differences between the two fields. Frank Cullen (1995) gives a more recent account in describing three characteristics that define criminal justice as a distinct discipline. Professor Cullen is a former President of the Academy of Criminal Justice Sciences, which is the other major professional association for crime researchers.

### A Definition of Criminal Justice

First, criminal justice is a social science discipline. While criminal justice began as a technical, pre-professional, or vocational program frequently taught at junior and community colleges, it has evolved into a popular social science discipline at many 4-year colleges and universities.

Second, criminal justice is a discipline with the distinctive hallmarks of an academic discipline, including the following:

- Distinct departments or programs, whose curricula are instructed fully by criminal justice faculty.
- Ph.D. programs dedicated to the creation of criminal justice knowledge and to the scholarly training of researchers, most of whom will assume academic positions.
- Numerous scholarly journals dedicated exclusively to the publication and transmission of criminal justice knowledge.
- Separate professional organizations dedicated to the dissemination of criminal justice knowledge through scholarship and education.
- A rapidly expanding knowledge base, which increasingly is produced by scholars trained by or working in departments of criminal justice.
- A large student population that defines itself as "criminal justice majors."
- Faculty whose academic identity is criminal justice. (Cullen, 1995, p. 3)

Third, Cullen insists that criminal justice is not simply the discrete compilation of insights drawn from scholars in different disciplines, nor a specialty or sub-field of any social science discipline. Criminal justice scholars can learn much from related disciplines such as sociology, psychology, political science, and history, but the unique task of criminal justice faculty is to integrate and evaluate these contributions and apply them to fashioning an understanding of crime (Cullen, 1995).

Cullen describes his views as "somewhat idiosyncratic," and not put forth as the "accepted wisdom of the field." His description does, however, contain much of what seems central to the discipline. The fact that the description is directed toward other academicians shows the difficulties new disciplines face in acquiring academic legitimation. Such reluctance has not, however, prevented the growth of criminal justice programs. The 1997-1998 *Guide to Graduate Programs in Criminal Justice and Criminology* (Academy of Criminal Justice Sciences, 1997) lists 114 graduate programs and 23 doctoral programs.

With respect to secondary data, the appearance and growth of criminal justice did more than simply increase the number of possible users. Though membership information for previous years was not available, by April 30, 1999, there were 2,154 paid members of the Academy of Criminal Justice Sciences. While sociological criminology has traditionally focused on the etiology of crime, criminal justice makes claims of being multidisciplinary as well as focusing on the operation of the criminal justice process. Thus, crime researchers count among their members people with a variety of backgrounds: political science, psychology, history, economics, and geography, to name a few. In addition, the focus on the criminal justice process means teaching and doing research on the structure and operation of police, courts, and corrections, as well as evaluating ways that agencies can be more effective in delivering services. Thus, accompanying the growth in numbers has been an increase in the number of crime researchers with backgrounds in other disciplines, as well as researchers interested in the structure, operations, and evaluation of components of the criminal justice process. All of the latter leads to a larger pool of possible secondary data users.

## Reducing the Schlepping Factor

According to the dictionary, *schlepping* is a Yiddish word referring to a tedious journey or to carry slowly, awkwardly, or tediously. Compared to the present, research a bare 25 years ago involved a great deal of schlepping. A very large amount of time during that period was devoted to tasks that had little to do directly with thinking about research designs, constructing indicators, analyzing data, and interpreting results. The time was devoted to getting material together to do the preceding; it was as if a carpenter were going to build a house, but first had to find and clear a location, dig the basement, truck all the material to the site, and only then begin construction.

Secondary data archives were small; requests resulted in a reel of tape that had to be mounted and read on a large mainframe computer, and the available software might or might not be compatible with the data set. For many students, secondary data meant a major professor gave permission to use part of his or her funded data set for a dissertation or thesis. With a research idea in mind, a tedious search through the library card catalog and annual volumes of research abstracts could, by itself, take several weeks. This was followed by a period of intense reading and thinking about how the available data set could be used to address one or more substantive issues uncovered by the literature search.

Analysis meant weeks and months in some computer center feeding SPSS batch programs to the mainframe, examining the results, correcting errors, resubmitting the job, and, eventually, submitting new ones. The preference of researchers was to work at night and into the early morning hours because the mainframe had fewer jobs to process, speeding the turnaround considerably. Turnaround time of 20 to 30 minutes from submission to printout was considered rapid progress.

Given this brief historical description of secondary data analysis, it is easier to understand why the amount of research completed pales in comparison to the amount that could have been done. Thankfully, for those currently interested in analyzing large data sets, we live in an age of computers. Beginning with Hyman's (1972) book, the history of secondary data use and analysis closely parallels the rise of the use of computers. Computers have made it possible to store large data sets, to make these data sets available to others, and to perform complex data analysis.

There are several software packages available for use in data analysis. The desktop version of SPSS, for example, provides all of the flexibility in managing, transforming, and analyzing data available in mainframe versions (with immediate turnaround). Statistical techniques in the standard package range from the usual bivariate techniques to many multivariate approaches such as ANOVA; multiple, logistic, and probit regression; factor analysis; discriminant function analysis; cluster analysis; and techniques for survival analysis. Statistical analyses can also be done by spreadsheets such as Excel, Lotus, and QuatroPro. Many statistical packages also include a capacity to generate charts, graphs, and a variety of graphical displays. The proliferation and evolution of increasingly sophisticated software for data analysis portends a bright future for secondary data analysis.

The next major change in using secondary data, already under way, is the development of the capacity to construct data sets on-line to suit the specific needs of researchers (see Chapter 2). When this capacity is joined to statistical analysis techniques for the data set constructed, future researchers will need access to only a computer and a modem to answer a variety of research questions.

## The Re-Emergence of the Independent Researcher

Citizens of the United States love their technology. Like most lovers, they tend to attribute characteristics to the object of affection that simply do not exist. In the case of technology, there is a tendency to believe that profound technological changes will somehow lead everyone to a quality of life that was previously unattainable. From automobiles to the Internet, freedom, wisdom, wealth, health, and a long life were promised at the outset.

The types of independent researchers discussed below were barely possible before the advent of sophisticated personal computers and the Internet. While a discussion of their re-emergence sounds an optimistic note, we know from previous history that technological changes have not been uniformly for the better and frequently have gone in unexpected directions.

In a 1963 article in the *American Behavioral Scientist,* Barney Glaser explored the relationship of secondary data to basic research by independent researchers. In this final section, I propose to reexamine these ideas because of the increased capacity to use secondary data. While Glaser focuses on sociological contributions to kn wledge, what he has to say is equally applicable to criminology and criminal justice.

The independent researcher "is one who engages in research is a personal venture, often on free time, (1) to satisfy his own curiosity, (2) to fulfill a desire to contribute to sociological knowledge, and (3) to do both in conformity with his own conception of a scientist's standard" (Lee, 1961, p. 159, cited in Glaser, 1963, p. 11). The image of a researcher drawn by Glaser is that of a "lone scholar" portrayed by Robert Merton (1957) and that of a scientist with a "calling" described by Max Weber (1946b). The major problem, Glaser suggests, is how to mobilize resources to accomplish some basic research.

Glaser discusses four types of independent researchers for whom easy access to secondary data can be enormously beneficial: team member, teacher, student, and the otherwise-employed sociologist. A fifth type is added: the enterprising citizen.

## The Team Member

The analysis of secondary data is a way that the independent researcher can step into the division of labor and provide benefits for himself or herself, the research team, and criminal justice. First, with respect to original ideas, Glaser suggests that original ideas may be sidetracked by "committee thinking" in team research and by team members with more power and influence. Glaser points out that secondary data analysis by individual team members and people who are not members of the team becomes a way of exploring data in an original fashion, free of the constraints and pressures of team research.

Second, by definition the independent researcher has few resources. But, Glaser notes, the costs of data collection are beyond the scope of independent researchers, not the costs of data analysis.

What is worth noting in his essay is that independent researchers may be limited in their exploration of secondary data because of constraints that existed at the time. For instance, he suggests that not only may team members engage in secondary analysis on their own, but it may be possible for others not connected with team research to do so. Perhaps a novel idea at the time, but present archival systems and the requirement of funding agencies that data from projects be placed in archives renders the question of outsiders using data moot.

The central conclusion is that secondary data make it possible for persons to do original and creative research that would be impossible otherwise. Increased ease of access to secondary data makes these conclusions even more relevant today.

## Teachers

Typically, full-time teachers are more adept at analysis than data collection. Because their data collection experience may be limited to their dissertation, it is a better use of teachers' precious time to make use of high-quality secondary data sets. In addition, use of secondary data permits teachers to pursue more than one publishable contribution.

## Students

Students are a third type of independent researcher. Graduate students have few or no funds to support any type of data collection, and it is unlikely they would obtain external funding, by themselves, in any large amounts. Funding for using secondary data can come from a variety of sources, but the three most applicable to researchers include (a) self-funding, (b) funding from grants or contracts, and (c) linking into existing major projects.

Self-funding refers to conducting secondary data analysis using the existing resources available to the researcher. For students, these resources take the form of free use of computers for data processing, libraries, and the borrowing of expertise from faculty members. There are additional opportunities for students in internships in relevant criminal justice agencies. Many governmental agencies have research units to carry out internal research, and all agencies collect records, data, and statistics.

Funding for secondary data analysis may also come from research grants, contracts, or both. Given the expense of obtaining data, there has been a growing consensus that secondary data analysis should be encouraged. As a result, federal agencies such as the National Institute of Justice and the National Science Foundation have small funding programs for the analysis of secondary data.

A final avenue of funding comes from linking into existing major projects. This requires an awareness of ongoing projects as well as the potential for collaboration. A student might offer to analyze portions of data in novel ways or hook up with a researcher to address mutual problems of common interest. Hakim (1987) notes that this "approach imposes most restrictions on the research design, since much will depend on the nature of the existing project and on the arrangements offered for linking into it" (p. 163).

Clearly there is a wide variety of opportunities to use secondary data when graduate students are faced with the problem of doing a dissertation or thesis. In my experience, the decision of graduate students to collect primary data is baffling in many instances. If the graduate student's goal is to complete a dissertation or thesis and become gainfully employed as soon as possible, collecting primary data with few funds and limited time is a high-risk venture. A better alternative is collecting data from official records, although, as noted in Chapter 4 and Chapter 5, much time can be lost unless data collection is carefully planned.

An opposing argument is that graduate students need the learning experience of collecting their own data, but it is difficult to see what useful knowledge for the future is gained by learning how to collect data with no funds and limited time. In addition, graduate students are increasingly expected to graduate with one or more publications to their credit. Being able to publish a thesis or dissertation is much more likely if high-quality data are used, whether they come from existing archives, official statistics, or are extracted from official records. In short, I am suggesting that the use of secondary data offers more positive benefits and fewer costs than do efforts to collect primary data. Perhaps archiving organizations can increase the use of secondary data among graduate students by targeting them in their public relations and advertising efforts.

## The Otherwise-Employed Sociologist

By the "otherwise-employed" sociologist, Glaser is referring to persons who are in staff or administrative positions. Accomplishing some basic research may have consequences for deans, vice presidents, and presidents—people who are somewhat removed from the direct activity of their discipline—that are similar to those associated with belonging to a professional association and receiving its journal. Engaging in a secondary analysis would maintain their professional self-image as scientists participating in the prestigious world of social research (Glaser, 1963, p. 14).

In addition, using secondary data to make research contributions can potentially provide a path back into teaching or research from other employment. Continuing to do research in addition to administrative duties helps to maintain the person's research credibility as well as prevent the loss of contributions from a person who may be a very creative scholar.

## The Enterprising Citizen

As noted, secondary data analysis is possible for any person who has the necessary interest, time, resources, and skills—all of which are attainable through independent effort. Certainly, many citizens have an interest in crime and criminal justice policies and may have time to do appropriate secondary data analysis. With the advent of distance learning possible through the Internet, and the ease and availability of databases and statistics, the day may soon arrive when the primary debaters over the proper interpretation of data are citizens.

## A Final Note

The proliferation and ease of access of secondary data may address a problem of which Glaser was unaware. As the United States moved to a more conservative political and social climate in the 1970s, the prestige of social science and the credibility of experts of various types declined. Federal funding agencies began to reflect the priorities of their political masters and needs of practitioners in the field. This has led to the funding of relatively narrow areas of inquiry that have, by and large, ignored basic research questions.

Unfortunately, elected representatives frequently appear to evaluate criminal justice initiatives by their contribution to re-election possibilities. Moreover, the future influence of practitioners on crime research is also uncertain. Given the problems faced by contemporary criminal justice, it is difficult to know whether practitioners have the relevant insights to appropriately inform funding decisions. An increase in the use of secondary data has the potential to provide a means to address questions that may not otherwise get answered. This alternative does not guarantee better results, but it does offer one of the few structured opportunities for exploring new ideas.

## Note

1. My thanks to Sarah Hall, Administrator, American Society of Criminology, for making membership information available.

# REFERENCES

Abt Associates. (1984). *Final draft of interim report national UCR conference.* Cambridge, MA: Abt Associates.

Academy of Criminal Justice Sciences. (1997). *Guide to graduate programs in criminal justice and criminology 1997-1998.* Highland Heights, KY: Academy of Criminal Justice Sciences.

Adler, A. R. (1995). *Litigation under the federal open government laws.* Washington, DC: American Civil Liberties Union.

Adler, F., Mueller, G. O. W., & Laufer, W. S. (1991). *Criminology* (3rd ed.). Boston: McGraw-Hill.

Akiyama, Y., & Rosenthal, H. M. (1990). The future of the Uniform Crime Reporting Program: Its scope and promise. In D. L. MacKenzie, P. J. Baunach, & R. R. Roberg (Eds.), *Measuring crime: Large-scale, long-range efforts* (pp. 49-74). Albany: State University of New York Press.

Alvarez, A. (1992). Trends and patterns of justifiable homicides: A comparative analysis. *Violence and Victims, 7*(4), 347-356.

Archer, D., & Gartner, R. (1984). *Violence & crime in cross-national perspective.* New Haven, CT: Yale University Press.

Babbie, E. R. (1986). *The practice of social research.* Belmont, CA: Wadsworth.

Bailey, K. D. (1994a). *Methods of social research* (4th ed.). New York: Free Press.

Bailey, K. D. (1994b). *Typologies and taxonomies: An introduction to classification techniques.* Thousand Oaks, CA: Sage.

Baker, T. L. (1999). *Doing social research* (3rd ed.). Boston: McGraw-Hill.

Baldus, D. C., Pulaski, C. A. J., & Woodworth, G. (1983). Comparative review of death sentences: An empirical study of the Georgia experience. *Journal of Criminal Law and Criminology, 74,* 661-753.

Baldus, D. C., Pulaski, C. A. J., & Woodworth, G. (1986). Arbitrariness and discrimination in the administration of the death penalty: A challenge to state supreme courts. *Stetson Law Review, 15,* 133-261.

Barzun, J., & Graff, H. F. (1985). *The modern researcher.* Fort Worth, TX: Harcourt Brace Jovanovich.

Baunach, P. J. (1990). State prisons and inmates: The census and survey. In D. L. MacKenzie, P. J. Baunach, & R. R. Roberg (Eds.), *Measuring crime: Large-scale, long-range efforts* (pp. 119-141). Albany: State University of New York Press.

Bennett, R. A., & Marshall, I. H. (1979). Criminal justice education in the United States: A profile. *Journal of Criminal Justice, 7,* 147-172.

Biderman, A. D., & Lynch, J. P. (1991). *Understanding crime incidence statistics: Why the UCR diverges from the NCS.* New York: Springer.

Biderman, A. D., & Reiss, A. J., Jr. (1967). On exploring the "dark figure" of crime. *Annals of the American Academy of Political and Social Science, 374,* 1-15.

Black, D. J. (1970). Production of crime rates. *American Sociological Review, 35,* 733-748.

Block, C. R. (1993). Lethal violence in the Chicago Latino community. In A. V. Wilson (Ed.), *Homicide: The victim/offender connection* (pp. 267-342). Cincinnati, OH: Anderson.

Block, C. R., & Block, R. (1997). *Homicides in Chicago, 1965-1995* (ICPSR 6399). Ann Arbor, MI: Inter-university Consortium for Political and Social Research.

Borg, W. R., & Gall, M. D. (1979). *Educational research.* New York: Longman.

Bottomley, K. (1979). *Criminology in focus: Past trends and future prospects.* Oxford, UK: Martin Robertson.

Bottomley, K., & Coleman, C. (1981). *Understanding crime rates.* Farnbourough, Hampshire, UK: Gower.

Bottomley, K., & Pease, K. (1986). *Crime and punishment: Interpreting the data.* Philadelphia: Open University Press.

Bowers, W., & Pierce, G. (1980). Arbitrariness and discrimination under post-Furman capital statutes. *Crime and Delinquency, 74,* 1067-1100.

Bulmer, M. (1984). Why don't sociologists make more use of official statistics? In M. Bulmer (Ed.), *Sociological research methods: An introduction* (pp. 131-153). New Brunswick, NJ: Transaction Books.

Bureau of Justice Statistics. (1998). *Criminal victimization, 1997* (NCJ-173385). Washington, DC: U.S. Department of Justice.

Burgess, R. G. (1984). *In the field: An introduction to field research.* London: George Allen & Unwin.

Campbell, D. T., & Ross, L. T. (1980). The Connecticut crackdown on speeding: Time-series data in quasi-experimental analysis. In S. Talarico (Ed.), *Criminal justice research: Approaches, problems, and policy.* Cincinnati, OH: Anderson.

Cantor, D., & Cohen, L. E. (1980). Comparing measures of homicide trends: Methodological and substantive differences in the vital statistics and Uniform Crime Report time series (1933-1975). *Social Science Research, 9,* 121-145.

Cardarelli, A. P. (Ed.). (1997). *Violence between intimate partners: Patterns, causes, and effects.* Boston: Allyn & Bacon.

Cecil, S., & Griffin, E. (1985). The role of legal policies in data sharing. In S. E. Fienberg, M. E. Martin, & M. L. Straf (Eds.), *Sharing research data* (pp. 148-198). Washington, DC: National Academy Press.

Champion, D. J. (1993). *Research methods for criminal justice and criminology.* Englewood Cliffs, NJ: Prentice Hall.

Cicourel, A. V. (1968). *The social organization of juvenile justice.* London: Heinemann.

Clarke, R. V., & Felson, M. (Eds.). (1993). *Routine activity and rational choice* (Vol. 5). New Brunswick, NJ: Transaction Publishing.

Cohen, J., & Cohen, P. (1983). *Applied multiple regression/correlation analysis for the behavior sciences* (2nd ed.). Hillsdale, NJ: Lawrence Erlbaum.

Cohen, L. E., & Felson, M. (1979). Social change and crime rate trends: A routine activity approach. *American Sociological Review, 44,* 588-608.

Comment. (1982-1983). Out of the sunshine and into the shadows: Six years of misinterpretation of the personal privacy exemption of the Kentucky Open Records Act. *Kentucky Law Journal, 71,* 823-847.

Conrad, J. P., & Myren, R. A. (1979). *Two views of criminology and criminal justice: Definitions, trends, and the future* (A Report for the Joint Commission on Criminology and Criminal Justice Education and Standards). Chicago: University of Illinois at Chicago Press.

Corwin, M. (1997). *The killing season: A summer inside an LAPD homicide division.* New York: Simon & Schuster.

Cullen, F. (1995). Fighting back: Criminal justice as an academic discipline. *ACJS Today, 13,* 1, 3.

Dale, A., Arber, S., & Procter, M. (1988). *Doing secondary analysis.* London: Unwin Hyman.

*Deitchman v. Squibb & Sons,* 740 F.2d 556 (7th Cir. 1984).

*Dept. of Justice v. Reporters Committee for Freedom of the Press,* 489 U.S. 749, 780 (1989).

*Dunns v. Bureau of Prisons,* 804 F.2d 1088, 1096 (D.C. Cir. 1986).

Durkheim, E. (1951). *Suicide: A study in sociology* (John A. Spaulding, George Simpson, Trans.). New York: Free Press.

Elliott, D. S. (1995). *Lies, damn lies, and arrest statistics.* Paper presented at the American Society of Criminology, Boston.

Elliott, D. S., & Ageton, S. S. (1980). Reconciling race and class differences in self-reported and official estimates of delinquency. *American Sociological Review, 45,* 95-110.

Emerson, R. M. (1983). Introduction. In R. M. Emerson (Ed.), *Contemporary field research: A collection of readings* (pp. 175-189). Boston: Little, Brown.

Ennis, P. H. (1967, June). Crime, victims, and the police. *Trans-Action,* pp. 36-44.

Federal Bureau of Investigation. (1992). *Uniform Crime Reporting handbook* (National Incident-Based Reporting System edition). Washington, DC: Author.

Federal Bureau of Investigation. (1996). *Crime in the United States—1995 Uniform Crime Reports.* Washington, DC: Government Printing Office.

Felson, M. (1998). *Crime and everyday life* (2nd ed.). Thousand Oaks, CA: Pine Forge Press.

Felson, M., & Cohen, L. E. (1980). Human ecology and crime: A routine activity approach. *Human Ecology, 8,* 389-406.

Finifter, B. M. (1975). Replication and extension of social research through secondary analysis. *Social Science Information, 14,* 119-153.

Flewelling, R. L., & Williams, K. R. (1999). Categorizing homicides: The use of disaggregated data in homicide research. In M. D. Smith & M. A. Zahn (Eds.), *Homicide: A sourcebook of social research* (pp. 96-106). Thousand Oaks, CA: Sage.

*Forsham v. Harris,* 445 U.S. 169, 183 (1980).

Frankfort-Nachmias, C., & Nachmias, D. (1996). *Research methods in social relations* (5th ed.). New York: St. Martin's.

Franklin, J. D., & Bouchard, R. F. (1995). *Guidebook to the freedom of information and privacy acts.* Deerfield, IL: Clark, Boardman, Callahan.

Futrell, M., & Roberson, C. (1988). *An introduction to criminal justice research.* Springfield, IL: Charles C Thomas.

Fyfe, J. J. (Ed.). (1982). *Readings on police use of deadly force.* Washington, DC: Police Foundation.

Garofalo, J. (1990). The National Crime Survey, 1973-1986: Strengths and limitations of a very large data set. In D. L. MacKenzie, P. J. Baunach, & R. R. Roberg (Eds.), *Measuring crime: Large-scale, long-range efforts* (pp. 75-96). Albany: State University of New York Press.

Gartner, R. (1997). Crime: Variations across cultures and nations. In C. Ember & M. Ember (Eds.), *Cross-cultural research for social science.* Englewood Cliffs, NJ: Prentice Hall.

Geerken, M. R. (1994). Rap sheets in criminological research: Consideration and caveats. *Journal of Quantitative Criminology, 10,* 3-21.

Geller, W. (1982). Deadly force: What we know. *Journal of Police Science and Administration, 10,* 151-177.

Gelles, R. J., & Straus, M. A. (1988). *Intimate violence.* New York: Simon & Schuster.

Gillespie, C. K. (1989). *Justifiable homicide: Battered women, self-defense, and the law.* Columbus: Ohio State University Press.

Glaser, B. G. (1963). The use of secondary analysis by the independent researcher. *American Behavioral Scientist, 6,* 11-14.

Gottfredson, D. M. (1999). *Exploring criminal justice: An introduction.* Los Angeles: Roxbury.

Gottfredson, M. R., & Gottfredson, D. M. (1988). *Decision making in criminal justice: Toward the rational exercise of discretion:* New York: Plenum.

Gove, W. R., Hughes, M., & Geerken, M. (1985). Are Uniform Crime Reports a valid indicator of index crimes? An affirmative answer with some minor qualifications. *Criminology, 23,* 451-501.

Griffiths, D., Irvine, J., & Miles, I. (1979). Social statistics: Towards a radical index. In J. Irvine, I. Miles, & J. Evans (Eds.), *Demystifying social statistics* (pp. 339-381). London: Pluto.

Gross, S. R., & Mauro, R. (1984). Patterns of death: An analysis of racial disparities in capital sentencing and homicide victimization. *Stanford Law Review, 37,* 27-153.

Gustavson, C. G. (1955). *A preface to history.* New York: McGraw-Hill.

Hagan, F. E. (1993). *Research methods in criminal justice and criminology.* Englewood Cliffs, NJ: Prentice Hall.

Hagan, F. E. (1997). *Research methods in criminal justice and criminology* (4th ed.). Boston: Allyn & Bacon.

Hakim, C. (1982a). Secondary analysis and the relationship between official and academic social research. *Sociology, 16,* 12-28.

Hakim, C. (1982b). *Secondary analysis in social research: A guide to data sources and methods with examples.* London: Unwin Hyman.

Hakim, C. (1983). Research based on administrative records. *Sociological Review, 31,* 489-519.

Hakim, C. (1987). *Research design: Strategies and choices in the design of social research.* London: Allen & Unwin.

Harries, K. D. (1989). Homicide and assault: A comparative analysis of attributes in Dallas neighborhoods, 1981-1985. *The Professional Geographer, 41,* 29-38.

Hawkins, D. F. (1999). What can we learn from data disaggreation? The case of homicide and African Americans. In M. D. Smith & M. A. Zahn (Eds.), *Homicide: A sourcebook of social research* (pp. 195-210). Thousand Oaks, CA: Sage.

Hindess, M. J. (1973). *The use of official statistics: A critique of positivism and ethnomethodology.* London: Macmillan.

Hood, R., & Sparks, R. (1970). *Key issues in criminology.* New York: McGraw-Hill.

Hyman, H. H. (1972). *Secondary analysis of sample surveys: Principles, procedures, and potentialities:* New York: John Wiley.

Illinois State Police. (1995). *Crime in Illinois—1994.* Springfield: State of Illinois.

Irvine, J., Miles, I., & Evans, J. (1979). *Demystifying social statistics.* London: Pluto.

Jacob, H. (1984). *Using published data: Errors and remedies.* Beverley Hills, CA: Sage.

Jarvis, J. P. (1992). The National Incident-Based Reporting System and its application to homicide research. In C. R. Block & R. Block (Eds.), *Questions and answers in lethal and non-lethal violence* (pp. 81-85). Washington, DC: Government Printing Office.

*John Doe Agency v. John Doe Corp,* 493 U.S. 146, 155 (1989).

Johnson, J. M. (1975). *Doing field research.* New York: Free Press.

Johnson, J. M. (1983). Trust and personal involvements in fieldwork. In R. M. Emerson (Ed.), *Contemporary field research: A collection of readings* (pp. 203-215). Boston: Little, Brown.

Jupp, V. (1989). *Methods of criminological research.* London: Unwin Hyman.

Kiecolt, K. J., & Nathan, L. E. (1985). *Secondary analysis of survey data.* Beverley Hills, CA: Sage.

Kitsuse, J. I., & Cicourel, A. V. (1963). A note on the uses of official statistics. *Social Problems, 11,* 131-139.

Kleck, G. (1988). Crime control through the private use of armed force. *Social Problems, 35,* 1-21.

Klein, M. W., Maxson, C. L., & Miller, J. (Eds.). (1995). *The modern gang reader.* Los Angeles: Roxbury.

Kraus, J. F., Sorenson, S. B., & Juarez, P. D. (Eds.). (1988). *Research conference on violence and homicide in Hispanic communities.* Los Angeles: UCLA Publication Services.

*Kurzon v. Dept. of Health and Human Serv.,* 649 F.2d 65 (1st Cir. 1981).

Little, R. J. A., & Rubin, D. B. (1987). *Statistical analysis with missing data.* New York: John Wiley.

Little, R. J. A., & Rubin, D. B. (1989). The analysis of social science data with missing values. *Sociological Methods and Research, 18,* 292-326.

Little, R. J. A., & Schenker, N. (1995). Missing data. In G. Arminger, C. Clogg, & M. Sobel (Eds.), *Handbook of statistical modeling for the social and behavioral sciences* (pp. 39-75). New York: Plenum.

Martinez, R. (1997). Homicide among Miami's ethnic groups: Anglos, blacks, and Latinos in the 1990s. *Homicide Studies, 1,* 17-34.

Maxfield, M. G., & Babbie, E. (1998). *Research methods for criminal justice and criminology* (2nd ed.). Belmont, CA: West/Wadsworth.

May, R. W. (1982). Discriminant analysis in cluster analysis. In H. C. Hudson & Associates (Eds.), *Classifying social data* (pp. 39-55). San Francisco: Jossey-Bass.

Merton, R. K. (1957). *Social theory and social structure.* New York: Free Press.

Moore, J., & Pinderhughes, R. (Eds.). (1993). *In the barrios: Latinos and the underclass debate.* New York: Russell Sage.

Morn, F. T. (1980). *Academic disciplines and debates: An essay on criminal justice and criminology as professions in higher education* (A Report of the Joint Commission on Criminology and Criminal Justice Education and Standards). Chicago: University of Illinois at Chicago.

Morris, R., Sales, B., & Berman, J. (1981). Research and the Freedom of Information Act. *American Psychologist, 36,* 819-822.

Mulvihill, D. J., & Tumin, M. M. (1969). *Crimes of violence* (National Commission on the Causes and Prevention of Violence, Vol. 11). Washington, DC: Government Printing Office.

National Institute of Justice. (1998). *Data resources of the National Institute of Justice* (11th ed.). Washington, DC: Government Printing Office.

*New York Times v. NASA,* 782 F. Supp. 628 (D.D.C. 1991).

O'Brien, R. M. (1985). *Crime and victimization data.* Beverley Hills, CA: Sage.

Paternoster, R., Brame, R., Bachman, R., & Sherman, L. W. (1997). Do fair procedures matter? The effect of procedural justice on spouse assault. *Law & Society Review, 31,* 163-204.

Poggio, E. C., Kennedy, S. D., Chaiken, J. M., & Carlson, K. E. (1985). *Blueprint for the future of the Uniform Crime Reporting Program: Final report of the UCR study.* Boston: Abt Associates.

Radelet, M. (1981). Racial characteristics and the imposition of the death penalty. *American Sociological Review, 46,* 918-927.

*Rainey v. Levitt,* 525 N.Y.S. 2d 551 (1988).

Rand, M. R. (1993). The study of homicide caseflow: Creating a comprehensive homicide dataset. *Questions and answers in lethal and non-lethal violence: Proceedings of the Second Annual Workshop of the Homicide Research Working Group* (pp. 103-118). Washington, DC: Government Printing Office.

Raymond, M. R. (1986). Missing data in evaluation research. *Evaluation and the Health Professions, 9,* 395-420.

Raymond, M. R., & Roberts, D. M. (1987). A comparison of methods for treating incomplete data in selection research. *Educational and Psychological Measurement, 47,* 13-26.

Regoeczi, W. C., Silverman, R. A., & Kennedy, L. W. (1996, November). *Predicting homicide clearances in Canada and the United States.* Paper presented at the American Society of Criminology, Chicago.

Reiss, A. J. (1971). *The police and the public.* New Haven, CT: Yale University Press.

Riedel, M. (1976). Discrimination in the imposition of the death penalty: A comparison of the characteristics of offenders sentenced pre-Furman and post-Furman. *Temple Law Quarterly, 49,* 261-283.

Riedel, M. (1990). Nationwide homicide datasets: An evaluation of UCR and NCHS data. In D. L. MacKenzie, P. J. Baunach, & R. R. Roberg (Eds.), *Measuring crime: Large-scale, long-range efforts* (pp. 175-205). Albany: State University of New York Press.

Riedel, M. (1993). *Stranger violence: A theoretical inquiry.* New York: Garland.

Riedel, M. (1998). *California homicides data file.* Carbondale: Southern Illinois University.

Riedel, M. (1999). Sources of homicide data. In M. D. Smith & M. Zahn (Eds.), *Homicide studies: A sourcebook of social research* (pp. 75-95). Thousand Oaks, CA: Sage.

Riedel, M., & Best, J. (1998). Patterns in intimate partner homicide: California, 1987-1996. *Homicide Studies, 2,* 305-320.

Riedel, M., & Jarvis, J. (1998). The decline of arrest clearances for criminal homicide: Causes, correlates, and third parties. *Criminal Justice Policy Review, 9,* 279-305.

Riedel, M., & Rinehart, T. A. (1996). Murder clearances and missing data. *Journal of Crime and Justice, 19,* 83-102.

Riedel, M., Zahn, M., & Mock, L. (1985). *The nature and patterns of American homicide.* Washington, DC: Government Printing Office.

Ritter, H. (1986). *Dictionary of concepts in history.* New York: Greenwood.

Rubin, D. (1976). Inference and missing data. *Biometrika, 63,* 581-592.

Schatzman, L., & Strauss, A. L. (1973). *Field research: Strategies for a natural sociology.* Englewood Cliffs, NJ: Prentice Hall.

Schneider, V. W., & Wiersema, B. (1990). Limits and use of the Uniform Crime Reports. In D. L. MacKenzie, P. J. Baunach, & R. R. Roberg (Eds.), *Measuring crime: Large-scale, long-range efforts* (pp. 21-48). Albany: State University of New York Press.

Sellin, T. (1938). *Culture conflict and crime.* New York: Social Science Research Council.

Senna, J., & Siegel, L. (1996). *Introduction to criminal justice* (7th ed.). Minneapolis, MN: West.

Sherman, L. W., & Berk, R. A. (1984). The specified deterrent effects of arrest for domestic assault. *American Sociological Review, 49,* 261-272.

Sherman, L. W., Gartin, P. R., & Buerger, M. E. (1989). Hot spots of predatory crime: Routine activities and the criminology of place. *Criminology, 27,* 27-55.

Sherman, L. W., & Langworthy, R. H. (1979). Measuring homicide by police officers. *Journal of Criminal Law and Criminology, 70,* 546-560.

Silverman, R. A., & Kennedy, L. W. (1987). Relational distance and homicide: The role of the stranger. *Journal of Criminal Law and Criminology, 78,* 272-308.

Simon, D. (1991). *Homicide: A year on the killing streets.* Boston: Houghton Mifflin.

Simon, J. L. (1969). *Basic research methods in social science.* New York: Random House.

Skogan, W. G. (1976). Crime and crime rates. In W. G. Skogan (Ed.), *Sample surveys of victims of crime.* Cambridge, MA: Ballinger.

Skogan, W. G. (1981). *Issues in the measurement of victimization* (NCJ-74682). Washington, DC: Government Printing Office.

Smith, H. W. (1991). *Strategies of social research.* Fort Worth, TX: Holt, Rinehart & Winston.

*St. Paul's Benevolent Educational and Missionary Institute v. United States,* 506 F. Supp. 822 (N.D. Ga. 1980).

Stevens, S. S. (1951). Mathematics, measurement, and psychophysics. In S. S. Stevens (Ed.), *Handbook of experimental psychology.* New York: John Wiley.

Stewart, D. W. (1984). *Secondary research: Information sources and methods.* Beverley Hills, CA: Sage.

Tennenbaum, A. N. (1993). *Justifiable homicides by civilians in the United States, 1976-1990: An exploratory analysis.* Unpublished doctoral dissertation, University of Maryland, College Park.

Traugott, M. W. (1990). Using archival data for the secondary analysis of criminal justice issues. In D. L. MacKenzie, P. J. Baunach, & R. R. Roberg (Eds.), *Measuring crime: Large-scale, long-range efforts* (pp. 145-155). Albany: State University of New York Press.

*U.S. Dept. of Justice v. Tax Analysts,* 492 U.S. 136, 144 (1989).

*Washington Post Co. v. Dept. of HHS,* 690 F.2d 252, 263 (1982).

Weber, M. (1946a). Bureaucracy. In H. H. Gerth & C. W. Mills (Eds.), *From Max Weber: Essays in sociology* (pp. 196-244). New York: Oxford University Press.

Weber, M. (1946b). Science as a vocation. In H. H. Gerth & C. W. Mills (Eds.), *From Max Weber: Essays in sociology.* New York: Oxford University Press.

Wilks, S. S. (1932). Moments and distributions of estimates of population parameters from fragmentary samples. *Annals of Mathematical Statistics, 3,* 163-195.

Williams, K., & Flewelling, R. L. (1987). Family, acquaintance, and stranger homicide: Alternative procedures for rate calculations. *Criminology, 25,* 543-560.

Williams, K. R., & Pampel, F. (1998, November). *Intimacy and homicide: Compensating for missing information in the Supplementary Homicide Reports.* Paper presented at the annual meeting of the American Society of Criminology, Washington, D.C.

*Wojtczak v. Dept. of Justice,* 548 F.Supp. 143, 148 (E.D. Pa. 1982).

Wolfgang, M. E., Figlio, R. M., & Sellin, T. (1972). *Delinquency in a birth cohort.* Chicago: University of Chicago Press.

Wolfgang, M. E., & Riedel, M. (1973). Rape, judicial discretion, and the death penalty. *Annals of the American Academy of Political and Social Science, 407,* 119-133.

Zahn, M. A., & Riedel, M. (1983). National versus local data sources in the study of homicide: Do they agree? In G. P. Waldo (Ed.), *Measurement issues in criminal justice* (pp. 103-120). Beverley Hills, CA: Sage.

# WORLDWIDE WEB SITES

## (UPDATED: 9/2/99)

CDC Wonder
http://wonder.cdc.gov/Welcome.html

Chicago Homicide Codebook
http://www.icpsr.umich.edu/NACJD/archive.html

Data Analysis System
http://www.icpsr.umich.edu/NACJD/SDA/das.html

Data Resources of the National Institute of Justice
http://www.icpsr.umich.edu/ICPSR/About/Publications/NACJD/nij98.pdf

Federal Justice Statistics Program
http://fjsrc.urban.org/index.shtml

Harvard Project on Human Development
http://phdcn.harvard.edu/geninfo.htm

Henry A. Murray Research Center at Radcliffe College
http://www.radcliffe.edu/murray/index.htm

ICPSR and NACJD Users
http://www.icpsr.umich.edu/NACJD/top.html

Inter-university Consortium for Political and Social Research
http://www.icpsr.umich.edu/

The National Archive of Criminal Justice Data
http://www.icpsr.umich.edu/NACJD/

The National Center for Juvenile Justice
http://www.ncjj.org/

The National Data Archive on Child Abuse and Neglect
http://www.fldc.cornell.edu/

Statistical Analysis Centers
http://www.jrsa.org/

Supplementary Homicide Reports
http://www.icpsr.umich.edu/NACJD/ucr96.html#shr

UCR file on Offenses Known to the Police and Clearances by Arrest
http://www.icpsr.umich. edu/ NACJD/ucr96.html#okca

The UnCover Company
http://uncweb.carl.org/

United Nations Surveys of Crime Trends and Operations of Criminal Justice
Systems (1970-1994)
http://www.ifs.univie.ac.at/~uncjin/wcs.html

U.S. Census Bureau
http://www.census.gov/main/www/access.html

# AUTHOR INDEX

# SUBJECT INDEX

# ABOUT THE AUTHOR

**M**arc **Riedel** is Associate Professor for the Center of Crime, Delinquency, and Corrections at Southern Illinois University. He does research on prescribed and proscribed forms of violence. His articles on the death penalty and homicide have appeared in the *Annals of the American Academy of Political and Social Science, Journal of Criminal Law and Criminology,* and *Temple Law Quarterly.* His eighth book, *Stranger Violence: A Theoretical Inquiry,* was published in 1993. He has served on the Executive Council and as Vice President of the American Society of Criminology. In 1985, he received the Herbert A. Bloch award from the American Society of Criminology for outstanding service to the society and the profession.